EVIL BROTHERS

A TRUE CRIME STORY

A tough police investigator tracks down two serial rapist-killers
On a savage spree in Midwestern America.

Frank P. Stiles

Outskirts Press, Inc.
Denver, Colorado

Dedication

To the victims who perished and those who survived. May this book stand as a tribute to their strength, courage, and love for life. To the families of those who did not survive, may this book remind us not of the violence and pain they endured but, of the love and good memories they leave behind. For those who survived, may the strength that carried them through their terrifying ordeal remind them that they were spared for a reason and, that they have important things to accomplish.

To my children, Kevin, Carey, and Amy Stiles, who at times sacrificed the companionship a father knows they deserved, so I could pursue the bad guys. For the hours, days, and many, many nights I was working and not at home, I want them to know how much I appreciated their love, support, and understanding.

To my late sister Emmagene (Stiles) Pierce, who along with my deceased parents, Janie and Eugene Sr., raised me and taught me honor, respect, integrity, and sensitivity.

To my deceased older brothers, Eugene Jr., Bill, and Jerry, along with my living older brothers, Edward and Donald, who taught me family values, brotherly love, and how to fight for what is right and good.

To my loving wife, B.J. Stiles, who is my friend, confidante, and inspiration.

Acknowledgements

To all the Toledo police division officers, and surrounding police department officers, who dedicated their time and effort in assisting with the successful conclusion of these heinous homicides and crimes. To all the prosecutors who brought these cases to a rightful ending.

A special acknowledgment to Thomas Ross, former Toledo police detective and current Lucas County Prosecutor's Office investigator, for his hard work on many of these cases and for the loss of his wife's niece believed to be one of the victims in this series of homicide-rapes.

Cover art: Terry Cousino, Toledo Police forensic artist, crime scene investigator, and latent print examiner.

Journalist Jim Eckstrom and retired journalist and writer Tom Gearhart for their assistance during the writing of this book.

To my good friend Jerry Dirr, who was the first to read my rough draft and who gave me the encouragement to continue.

To John Robinson Block and the Toledo Blade, for some research information and photographs, obtained from their past newspaper morgue.

Last but not least, I want to acknowledge Julia R. Bates, Lucas County Prosecuting Attorney. It was she who in October 1997 contacted me after my retirement from the Toledo Police Division, with the idea of using the new technology of DNA. She suggested that we compare any blood and or semen evidence from the homicide and rape victims, back in 1980 and 1981, with suspects Anthony and Nathaniel Cook's DNA. I provided her with a list of potential victims

I had developed during my past investigations, including the arrest of Anthony Cook for the Peter Sawicki homicide and, DNA evidence was searched for and tested in those cases.

As a result of those tests, Anthony and Nathaniel Cook's DNA was positively confirmed with that of victim Sandra Podgorski. Tying the brothers to Sandra Podgorski's assault and rape, the brothers were arrested for the crimes committed against her and the homicide of her boyfriend, Thomas Gordon.

We later worked out a plea agreement with the Cook brothers and their attorneys, solving most of the remaining cases Anthony and Nathaniel Cook were suspected of committing in 1980 and 1981. As a result of this plea agreement we were able to bring closure to the surviving victims, and many family members of all the victims. Anthony Cook will be in prison for the remainder of his natural life. Nathaniel Cook was incarcerated for twenty years, and will not be eligible for parole until he has served the full twenty years.

Introduction

This is a true crime story about two serial killers, Anthony and Nathaniel Cook, and Frank Stiles, the police detective who tracked them down and put them in prison. While cruising in their beat-up pickup truck the Cook brothers terrorized the city of Toledo and Lucas County, Ohio, during the years 1980 and 1981. The story made national news. Nine murders and various rapes, robberies, and assaults were solved, with at least three other murders still under investigation. The brothers were night stalkers who preyed upon young white victims sitting in their cars or walking on the street.

One brother was arrested in 1981 for the murder of a businessman, the attempted murder and attempted rape of the man's daughter, and the robbery and attempted murder of the daughter's boyfriend but, it was not until1998 when DNA technology was able to identify both brothers as serial killers. As a result, Anthony and Nathaniel Cook confessed to their crimes, and most of the murders and assaults were solved.

Both brothers pleaded guilty in April of 2000 and are in prison, one for life and the other for at least 20 years.

Frank Stiles, the lead detective, takes readers through every step of the investigation, vividly describing the brutal abductions, rapes, and torturous murders of these young people.

The arrest and detailed confessions from the brothers lay bare the cold-bloodedness of the stalkers, and how calculated and premeditated the murders were carried out, with little evidence or witnesses.

Chapter 1

Evil Brothers

Anthony Haven Cook was born on March 9, 1949 to Marjorie and Hayes Cook II in Mobile, Ala, while the state was still struggling under segregation. It was a period when politicians found it difficult to get elected unless they were outspoken segregationists.

Marjorie was a devoted Christian and strict mother who made her children attend church and Sunday school. If any of the children neglected to go to church they were punished and restricted to the house.

The family fled Alabama and moved around – to California, Dayton, Columbus, Ohio and Toledo.

Migrating to Toledo in search of better jobs, Hayes Cook became an industrial crane operator and worked on cars part-time for a local garage.

Anthony's parents divorced in 1959 when Anthony was 9, leaving his unemployed mother to care for nine children. Cook's mother remarried and had two more children, but that marriage ended in divorce as well.

When Anthony's biological parents divorced, he showed resentment and became incorrigible. His younger brother of nine years, Nathaniel, looked up to his older brother as a father-like image.

Their brother, Hayes Cook III, would later be arrested for rape and sent to prison.

Anthony and his mother worked odd jobs to raise money for the family. Inheriting his father's skills, Anthony was good with his hands and could fix anything. He took toys apart and reassembled them without difficulty, later graduating to appliances, bicycles and cars. Anthony did poorly in school and attended a junior high school for boys with scholastic difficulties.

Struggling with depression and a hard life, Anthony experienced the trauma guns can cause when he shot himself while attempting suicide at age 16. He survived his self-inflicted gunshot wound and later in life went on to inflict pain and suffering on others.It was as though Anthony wanted them to feel his pain and so he developed an enjoyment of hurting and killing others. It would seem this was his way of getting back at society for the unhappy and painful life he felt he had been subjected to.

With little self-esteem, Anthony took to the streets at an early age. His street name was "Hawkeye" and his crimes grew from minor offenses to armed robbery.

Later, after dropping out of Scott High School at age 18, he was arrested for robbing a man at gun point. Within a week, he was involved in snatching an old woman's purse. Anthony was caught, and while locked up, the court ordered a psychological evaluation. The evaluation indicated he had trouble getting along with family and friends, and he was diagnosed with schizophrenia, a psychotic disorder characterized by loss of contact with his environment – having trouble functioning in everyday life.

On April 26, 1973, Anthony Cook was granted parole. While in prison he complained about the ill treatment he received from white guards and was quoted by family members as saying the white man was the enemy. Shortly after his release from prison, Anthony went on one of the bloodiest killing sprees in history. All of his victims would be white, which suggests it was his inner hatred of the white prison guards and his depressed and unhappy childhood that triggered his rage.

Most of the killings were committed by Anthony alone but, later, he would entice his younger brother Nathaniel to join in his evil deeds. Nathaniel's personality was different than Anthony's. During his adolescent years Nathaniel helped his mother around the house and with caring for his sisters. When not in Anthony's company, he was outgoing and got along well with friends and family, leading somewhat of a normal and productive life. He was a maintenance man for a habilitation group home for the mentally disabled and drove semi-trucks over the road hauling mostly steel. He was not known to get into serious trouble on his own, but appeared to be intrigued by Anthony's crime wave and stints in prison.

Anthony's first unsuspecting target would be that of 22-year-old Vicki Lynn Small - the bloodbath had just begun.

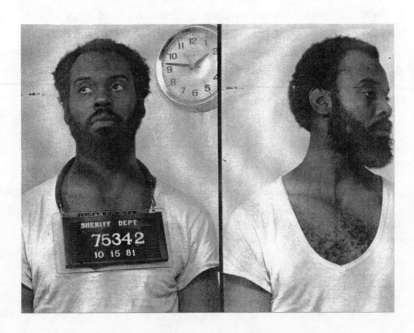

Police arrest photo of Anthony Cook

Police arrest photo of Nathaniel Cook

Anthony Cook's pickup truck used during the murders

Chapter 2
Vicki Lynn Small

T oledo's metropolitan area of 450,000 people is located in Lucas County, northwest Ohio, on Lake Erie. The fourth largest city in the state is known as the Glass City because of its glass development and manufacturing of auto windows, tableware products, industrial bottles, and other various types of glass. Many handmade intricate cut glass collector pieces, donated by Edward Drummond Libbey, are still on display in the Toledo Museum of Art, one of the country's top 10 museums, which was founded by Libbey in 1901. Libbey pioneered Toledo's glass industry when he opened the Libbey Glass Company in 1888 and the family endowments support the museum still.

The city is also recognized for its Toledo Zoo, and for the manufacturing of the Jeep vehicle, from World War II to the present. Police and protection is excellent, and the crime rate is average for a city of its size.

Ottawa Park, one of several parks in the Toledo area, is located in a residential section of Toledo. It is here that the story of the Cooks begins. It is here where the unimaginable became the imaginable. On the snowy morning of December 20, 1973, the first of a series of violent homicides and rapes was discovered. The crimes that began that morning would terrorize the city and county for years to come.

Vicki Lynn Small was a pretty 22-year-old with blonde hair and green eyes. Single, she was employed as a data entry clerk for Blue Cross of Northwest Ohio. She lived with her boyfriend, Robert Davis, in north Toledo. Vicki was an honors graduate of DeVilbiss High School and attended the University of Toledo. She was a young woman looking forward to a bright future.

On Dec. 19, Robert was to work the overnight shift at Chrysler Corp. in nearby Perrysburg. On this wintry night, Vicki called her longtime friend and co-worker, Heather Green. They decided to go out together.

At 9:30 p.m., Heather picked up Vicki in her small AMC Gremlin. It had been snowing all day and the weather made it difficult to drive.

Heather and Vicki enjoyed playing pinball machines, so they first drove to Jakey's Bar downtown. Jakey's was a colorful neighborhood hangout and was considered safe because it's where local police officers congregated after work. Cops could swap war stories and tell each other about things they had experienced – things they may have found difficult to tell their spouses or family members.

A story has been told that it was at Jakey's several years before where two out of town robbers barged into the bar carrying guns. Unfamiliar with the bar, the robbers announced their demand for money. The cops drew their guns and shot the would-be robbers. It sounded like World War II, and when the smoke cleared, one robber lay dead and the other seriously wounded.

Arriving at Jakey's on this night, Heather and Vicki opened the door and looked inside. Through the thick smoke, noise, and loud voices, they saw the machines were in use so they went to the bus station nearby to play the pinballs there. They played several games until a drunken man with long blond hair came in. He made them feel uneasy so they left.

Hungry, the pair decided to get a pizza. They drove to Little Caesars in the Westgate area, but it was closed, so they went to Gino's.

They finished eating and were leaving when they looked at the clock – 12:50 a.m. They decided to call it a night because they both had to be up at 6 a.m. for work.

As Heather was taking Vicki home, it became more difficult to drive due to the falling snow and freezing roadways.

As they drove down Cherry Street toward Vicki's home, Heather turned right near St. Vincent's Hospital. While she was maneuvering, the Gremlin became stuck in the snow a short distance from Vicki's house.

Heather tried to rock the car free, but it was no use. They were stuck.

A large green Pontiac with a black vinyl top appeared. In the car were two black men. The driver was 20 to 25 years old, 6 feet tall, 150 pounds, medium complexion, short hair and sideburns, wearing a light-colored shirt that was open at the neck, hip-length cloth jacket, and powder blue pants that were too short for him.

The passenger was 25 to 30 years old, stocky, with a medium afro, sunken eyes, and a mustache. He was wearing a dark coat with orange trim.

The men pulled up to their car and the driver hollered. "Do you need help?" "Yes," replied Heather. The men got out and approached the Gremlin. The driver told Heather and Vicki to get out of the car, then he slid into the car behind the wheel. Heather, Vicki, and the other man got behind Heather's car and tried to push it free.

They still could not dislodge the vehicle, so they went to the front of the car and pushed it back around the corner. Before they could totally free the car, a navy blue Chevrolet came to the intersection and one of the men motioned to the driver of the car that they needed a push. The driver pushed them free then left.

Heather was shocked to see Vicki get into the Pontiac with the two men. She followed, and when it stopped, the driver told her that they were going to take Vicki home. Heather then drove east on Cherry to her house.

Heather thought it was strange that Vicki would ride with two strangers, especially when she lived only a few blocks away.

When Heather got home, she called Vicki's apartment to make sure she had arrived safely. It was 2 a.m. and Vicki's boyfriend,

Robert, answered the telephone. Robert, who had stayed home from work because of the bad weather, had been wondering where Vicki was.

Heather told Robert about the two men helping them free her car from the deep snow, and about the men giving Vicki a ride home. Heather told Robert to call her as soon as Vicki got home. When she did not hear from him she again called. Vicki was still not home and he had not heard from her.

Worried for her friends' safety, Heather called the police and told them of Vicki's disappearance. Within a short time, Toledo Police Officers Phillip Wesley and Bruce Klinck came to her home. They took her report and told her to call if Vicki returned. She called Robert and told him that she had reported Vicki missing. By now, he too was very worried and upset.

At 5:25 a.m. Police Officers George Stanley and Duane Szewczykowski, were patrolling their district and traveling through Ottawa Park, heading east on Ottawa Parkway. They saw an object that looked like a piece of cardboard lying in the snow. As the officers got nearer and shined their flashlights on the object, they saw it was the body of a woman.

She appeared to be 18 to 22 years old and was lying in the snow, fully dressed with a white glove stuffed in her mouth. The woman was wearing a navy pea-coat with brass buttons, beige slacks with green patch pockets, a pullover polo shirt, mustard-colored knee socks, a pair of blue and maroon suede shoes with 2-inch heels, and a mustard-colored neck scarf tied in a bow. It turned out to be Vicki Small.

Where she had lain in the snow, the officers found a set of footprints leading north alongside the body. Her head was facing north with her legs drawn up toward her chest. There were other footprints around the body and tire tracks heading in an east-to-west direction near the body. The tire tracks were lightly covered with snow.

As the officers approached, they could see the woman was not breathing and when they checked her pulse they found none. The officers could see blood running down the right side of her head from an unknown wound. Crime scene technician Peter Hodak and crime laboratory supervisor Captain Edward Clancy were called to the scene along with the Lucas County coroner, Dr. Harry Mignerey. He pronounced the woman dead and the crime scene was processed. Photographs were taken, plaster tire impressions were made of the tire tracks, and the woman was transported to the Toledo Hospital morgue.

Heather was picked up at her home and taken to Toledo Hospital by the police. She broke down when shown the body of Vicki and could not bring herself to make an identification. The 19 year-old sister of Vicki, Rebecca Small, later identified the body.

When the autopsy was performed by Dr. Mignerey, he found Vicki died as a result of brain damage from four gunshot wounds to the head. Two other gunshot wounds were found to the heart and lungs. Vicki had a bruise on the left side of her upper lip and semen was identified in vaginal smears. There were powder burns on the head and clothing in the chest area, indicating Vicki was shot at close range. Ballistic test determined the weapon to be a 25 caliber pistol.

This homicide/rape appeared to be an isolated case because no other crimes with this modus operandi had occurred around this time – or would occur until years later.

No one had any idea that this would be the first of a series of rape/homicides due to resume more than six years later on May 14, 1980. No one had any idea that this series was prolonged because the killer, Anthony Cook, had been arrested after Vicki's murder, for robbing two people at gunpoint while walking on the street. Cook was in prison for the street robbery from July 26, 1974, until paroled on Nov. 13, 1979.

Anthony Cook's release from prison would be the restart of this series of rapes and homicides.

The series of victims over the next two years, would tragically take away the dreams, ambitions, and lives of those young people who had every reason and right to live. These young victims were not like some young people who were living on the edge or involved in criminal activity that would most likely end in some form of tragedy. The young victims in this series of rape and homicide cases were from average to affluent families. They had plans for their futures, a purpose to their lives, and a hunger to succeed.

These young people were not in the wrong place at the wrong time, they were in areas where they felt safe and should have been safe. One never knows what life has in store: "There but for the grace of God, go I."

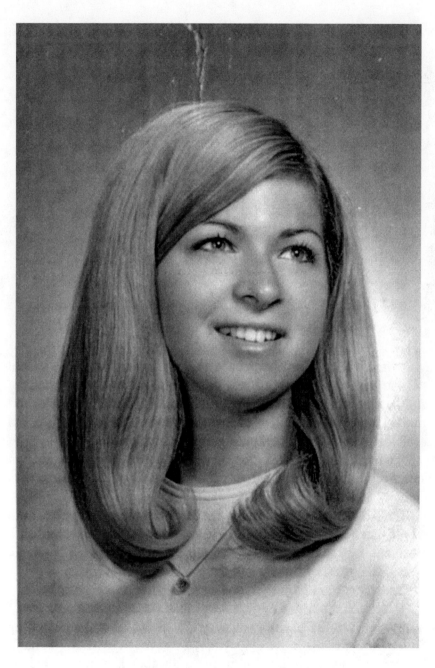

Victim Vicki Lynn Small

Chapter 3
Thomas Gordon and
Sandra Podgorski

I t wasn't long after Thomas Gordon graduated from high school that he took a factory job and was working toward a career in the automotive industry. Sandra Podgorski had finished high school and found employment. Neither of them was sure what to do in life, but both were considering continuing their education.

Thomas, 24, worked for Doehler Jarvis Technologies, an automotive die casting Company that did much of its business with General Motors.

Sandra, 18, was working for Plastex Industries, a recycler. Both Sandra and Thomas lived with their parents, trying to establish a financial base so they could afford a place of their own. The couple were quiet people who enjoyed the simple things in life.

They met months earlier, and began dating on a regular basis.

Sandra and her family lived on Utica Street in Toledo's lower north end. On the evening of May 13, 1980, Thomas picked up Sandra at her home in his Chevy Nova and they drove to Thomas's brothers for a visit. A little after midnight, they left and headed for Sandra's house.

It was dark and quiet when Thomas pulled up in front of Sandra's. The time was 12:30 a.m. They embraced and talked quietly about the evening and the future. The evening was slipping away when Sandra said, "Tom, it is late and I really should go inside."

As they kissed goodnight, a frightening sound broke the silence. The window glass on the passenger's side of the car, where Sandra was sitting, exploded in their faces.

Sandra was confronted with a rifle pointed at her face, held by a tall black man in his 20s, wearing an army jacket, blue jeans, and a red and white baseball cap. On the driver's side of the car, where Thomas sat, stood a black man of medium stature in his early 30s. The man had a full beard, mustache, and sideburns, and was wearing blue jeans, a dark jacket, and a beige stocking cap.

The couple was forced into the back seat. The man with the rifle got into the passenger seat while the other got behind the wheel.

Thomas Gordon pleaded with the attackers to take his money and his car but not to harm him or his girlfriend. The man with the gun said, "If you cooperate, we won't hurt you." The assailant driving the car drove to a nearby alley and made Thomas get out of the car. They tried to force him into the trunk but he pleaded with them not to. The men finally returned him to the back seat alongside Sandra. The assailant with the rifle returned to the passenger seat while the other drove the car.

Thomas was told to lay his head on Sandra's lap and she was told to rest her head on his shoulder. Even though Thomas and Sandra were told not to look up, they were able to catch glimpses of where they were at from time to time. They saw that they were on the expressway. Soon the driver of the car turned onto Central Avenue, away from Toledo.

They drove for about 30 minutes and ended up on a secluded country road with woods on one side and a plowed field on the other. Sandra saw a sign in front of them that read, "One Lane Bridge." There were no buildings or farmhouses in sight.

As the car stopped alongside the deserted road, Sandra's heart felt like it had stopped. Both Thomas and Sandra knew that they were in deep trouble.

The gunmen got out and took Thomas to the passenger side. The driver took his wallet, and then Thomas yelled "Oh, God, no," and ran into the plowed field. The other robber chased Thomas, and Sandra heard the horrifying sound of the rifle being fired, then heard Thomas scream, "Oh, my heart!" There was a pause, then the crack of three more shots.

The robber who stayed behind told Sandra to remove her clothes. He forced her from the car and made her lie on the ground at the top of a ditch. The man forced himself on Sandra and raped her. During this ordeal, Sandra prayed for the horror to stop.

After the rapist was through he crawled off her. Sandra was thankful he was done, but her torment had just begun. The robber with the rifle returned from shooting Thomas and waited on the driver's side while Sandra was being raped. When the first rapist was finished with her, the other then raped her.

When the assault was finally over, Sandra was forced to return to the rear seat and told to put her pants back on. As Sandra sat frozen and petrified she heard the killers talking. Sandra heard one say, "You can't leave him out there." She also heard one of the killers call the other "Tony." The killers entered the car and drove to a dirt road leading into the field where Thomas had been shot. The car was backed down this road a short distance to where Thomas's body lay. They opened the trunk of the car and threw him into the trunk like an old spare tire.

The killer who shot Thomas now became the driver while his partner, who had driven before, got into the back seat of the car with Sandra. She knew that the man now in the back seat with her was the one in charge. The bearded killer asked her her name and how old she was. She told him and he replied that he should have more sex with her but made no attempt to do so. It was as if he enjoyed torturing her.

The driver had driven in the direction of Toledo when Sandra felt a sharp pain in her right shoulder. She looked up and observed the killer's hand coming toward her with what appeared to be an ice-pick. He stabbed her in the neck and chest.

Sandra, though weak, fought to defend herself. She was able to wrestle the weapon from the killer's hand, but the driver pulled the car over and assisted his partner in getting the weapon back from Sandra. She was struck in the mouth and the killers forced the weapon from her. Once the killer in the back seat had the weapon back he again resumed stabbing Sandra in the chest, shoulders and head. The pain was excruciating and fear of death filled Sandra's mind.

Sandra realized that the only way to survive was to feign death. She pretended to be dead even though the pain was almost unbearable and she was choking on her own blood. She let her body go limp, struggling with the pain. It was all she could do to hold back from coughing and spitting up blood.

The stabber crawled to the front seat when he was satisfied she was dead. It seemed like forever before Sandra caught a glimpse of the intersection of Lagrange and Utica. She realized that they had finally gotten back to the area of her home where they had been abducted from. The car stopped and the killer who had stabbed her got out of the car and went to a dark-colored pickup truck with a white camper top.

The killer driving Thomas's car followed the pickup truck to a secluded dirt alley.

Sandra still lay in the back seat pretending to be dead. The driver got out of Thomas's car and approached the other killer, who by now had walked up to the rear of Thomas's car.

The killers opened the trunk, making sure Thomas was dead. She heard the killers talking and heard one of the killers say, "I don't think the bitch is dead."

Sandra felt the killers must have finally decided she was also dead because she then heard the doors to their vehicle slam shut and heard them drive away. She lay still for approximately 10 minutes until she felt safe that the killers were not going to return. Sandra forced her pain-wracked body up and out of the car, knowing she had to get help or die. She struggled through the alley and found a house a short distance away. It was here that she was able to get help and the police were called.

Police and emergency vehicles raced to the scene with lights flashing and sirens screaming. The sounds of the emergency vehicles arriving broke the stillness of the night while, alerting all that something serious and awful had occurred.

Although the pain continued there was a look of relief that covered Sandra Podgorski's face when she was loaded onto a gurney and placed into the rear of the ambulance. She was rushed to Riverside Hospital where she was treated for a punctured lung and six other stab wounds. Sandra was fortunate because none of her wounds were life threatening. The killers savage attempt to murder Sandra had failed – she would live to tell her horrible and terrifying story.

The scene where Sandra Podgorski and Thomas Gordon were left for dead was on McLean Street in the city's north end, an area some called dog-patch.

Uniform police crews and detectives soon saturated the area, along with search dogs, scientific investigation unit technicians, life squad personnel, and the coroner's investigator. The night air was a cool 50 degrees and it was overcast.

Police Officers Larry Scoble and Oscar Martinez were the first to arrive on the scene and while aiding and talking to Sandra, they were told that her boyfriend, Thomas Gordon, had been shot several times and was in the trunk of his car.

The officers looked into the car and observed that the keys were missing. They pried the trunk of the car open where they found Gordon's body.

The crime scene where the victim's car was recovered was processed for evidence. The police dogs were not much assistance because the killers fled in their pickup truck after abandoning the car. The coroner's investigator, Joseph Inman, directed that Gordon's body be transported to the Lucas County Morgue and the County Transport Service made the transfer. The Gordon car was towed to the Toledo Police Division's garage so that it could be processed for evidence.

Homicide detective Thomas Ross was dispatched to the abandoned car scene. He arrived, examined the scene and the available evidence, and conversed with Investigator Inman. Sandra had already been transported to Riverside Hospital for treatment so Detective Ross and Investigator Inman went to the hospital in an attempt to talk to her.

At the hospital, the investigators spoke with Sandra after she was treated, and she told her horrifying story. While she was describing the area in which she and Gordon had been taken and assaulted, Investigator Inman said he recognized this area and felt he could find the murder scene. He knew of a road where there was a one-lane bridge like the one Sandra described.

By the time Ross and Inman left the hospital it was daylight. They drove to the Rabb Road in Western Lucas County, where Inman suspected the crime may have occurred. While traveling on Rabb road they observed a one-lane bridge sign with woods on their left and a freshly plowed field to their right.

They observed that weeds along the edge of the road were matted down so they exited their car to investigate. They saw a farm truck in the field and a migrant farm worker from Texas by the name of Jose Valdez standing near the truck. Upon questioning, Valdez said that when he and other workers started work that morning at 7:30, they observed what appeared to be blood in the 12th and 13th rows of the field. They also observed what appeared to be drag marks and suspected that someone may have been injured or murdered.

Despite their suspicions of what the signs meant, the migrant workers had not bothered to call the Lucas County Sheriff's Department and just began their work. The workers began to plant cabbages and their tractors obliterated most of the crime scene. Tire impressions near the bloodstains were very faint and had been driven over with the heavy farm equipment. Toledo Police Scientific Investigation Unit technician Edwin Marok was summoned to the scene and he arrived along with Lucas County Sheriff Detective Gary Heil. Technician Marok photographed and prepared a sketch of the crime scene.

The Sheriff's Department was there because the murder and rape occurred in their jurisdiction. Victim Thomas Gordon was found to be the brother of Sheriff Deputy Walter (Wally) Gordon.

It was decided that the Toledo Police Division would be the lead investigatory agency because the abduction took place in the city. Police artist Robert Poiry worked with Sandra Podgorski and developed a sketch of the killers.

An autopsy showed the victim had been shot four or five times with a .22-caliber rifle. There was one entrance wound through the left side of the head and bullet fragments were recovered from the brain. Another entrance wound was found on the left side of the chest, with the bullet perforating the lungs, heart, aorta and superior vena cava. This bullet showed no signs of being fired at close range.

A third bullet wound was found to have entered the back of the body without evidence of close range firing on the surrounding skin. A fourth wound was found to be through the web of the left hand, between the thumb and the index finger. That wound showed evidence of near-contact firing. It is conceivable that the same bullet produced an atypical entrance wound under the chin. Thus, the deceased was shot at least four times. This bullet perforated the pharynx and esophagus. Small caliber bullet fragments, later determined by ballistic experts to have been fired from a Marlin .22 caliber rifle, were removed from those areas of the victim's body.

The composites of the killers drawn by police artist Robert Poiry were given to the uniform crews and area police departments in an attempt to identify the killers. Detective Poiry was not only a talented artist but a topnotch investigator as well.

Sandra's father Daniel took Sandra to live with his mother in fear the killers may return to silence her. He feared that after the killers discovered she had survived they would return in an attempt to eliminate the only witness. He sent his wife Bonnie and Sandra's two sisters to live with relatives in Kentucky for fear they might be harmed if the killers came for Sandra. Sandra remained in the Toledo area with her grandmother so she could assist the police with leads.

Alone at night, Daniel lay awake guarding his domain – waiting for the killers to return to the scene of the abduction. The killers never returned and eventually the family became one again..

Over the next four months no new productive leads were developed.

On Sept. 12th, Lucas County Sheriff Detective Gary Heil asked

Sandra to come to the Sheriff's Department and view photographs of black men who had been previously booked in the jail for various past charges. Due to the amount of time Sandra spent with the killers during her ordeal and by the description of the killers she gave, she would presumably be able to identify the killers.

Detective Heil reported that while Sandra was viewing mugshot books, she came upon a photograph of a man and she hesitated. He asked what the problem was and Sandra said her heart stopped when she saw this picture.

The photograph was that of George Eugene Talley, 22. Detective Heil had the photo lab technician, Deputy Trilby Cashin, look for a more recent photograph of the subject. She found one that was taken seven months later than the one initially viewed by Sandra.

Detective Heil showed Sandra the latest photograph and she stated that without a doubt this was the killer who had shot Thomas Gordon. The photograph identified matches her earlier description of the shooter and the man in the photograph was even wearing a green army jacket like the one Sandra had described when interviewed after the assault. Mr. Talley's age, height and weight, matched that of the killer.

Warrants were issued for Talley and he was arrested by Lucas County Sheriff Deputies, however after further investigation and a lie detector test given to Talley, Podgorski's identification proved erroneous and he was released. The killers were still on the prowl.

Sandra compares that horrible night with being branded with an iron; the killers burned their mark forever on her. She said the violence she and Thomas suffered has burdened her with a life of guilt that will remain with her for the rest of her life. The guilt she feels is the guilt of a survivor.

Victim – Thomas Gordon

Victim – Sandra Podgorski

Scene of Murder on Rabb Road

Thomas Gordon's abandoned car with Gordon in the trunk

Chapter 4

Connie Sue Thompson

E llyn Langenderfer and Kris Ulmer were good friends. Kris had been visiting Ellyn at her home on West Bancroft Street Jan. 17, 1981. Ellyn lived in the country and Kris lived in Toledo, but they were together this day. Both were 15 and both were in the 10th grade at Saint Ursula Academy, a Catholic school for girls. It was 3 p.m. when the girls decided to go outside. While they were playing and sledding on this cold, snowy day, they would make a frightening discovery.

The girls were sledding in the area of a concrete culvert which extended under the roadway from one side of Bancroft to the other. Langenderfer Road crosses Bancroft and the culvert is just east of Langenderfer. Ellyn lived just west of Langenderfer. As the girls rode their sleds down past the culvert, they looked under the road and into the culvert. Surrounded by the fresh snow, they saw the body of a woman lying in the shallow water. The body was exposed but partially frozen in a few inches of water.

The girls frantically ran to Ellyn's house where the Lucas County Sheriff's Department was summoned. Deputies responded and found the body, which was fully clothed. It appeared the body had been there before the snow fell, for there were no prints in the area. The body had been dragged inside the culvert and dumped face down.

The victim was a young white woman, around 20 years old. She was wearing blue jeans, a turquoise sweater and a white scarf. A black ski jacket with red trim was found on the ground near the body. Blood appeared to be on the jacket. The victim was wearing earrings and a ring on her finger.

Lucas County detectives and the coroner's investigator were called, and after the scene was processed for evidence, the body was removed to the morgue.

The body of this 18-year-old woman was found to be that of Connie Sue Thompson. She had been reported missing on Jan. 5 by her sister, Diane Willets. Miss Thompson's clothing was the same clothing described when she was reported missing. Connie Sue Thompson was a petite red-haired young woman; who had been living with her 33-year-old sister, Diane Willets, on Peck Street in north Toledo.

An autopsy was performed by assistant coroner Renate Fazekas, and the cause of death was determined to be the result of 43 stab wounds to the neck and chest area. The victim had been beaten about the face and upper body, stabbed, and strangled with an unknown ligature 1/16th of an inch wide.

Four stab wounds were to the left side of the neck, two were located on the right side of the chest, and 37 were located over the left side of the chest. The victim had been sexually assaulted, with semen being identified-vaginally and rectally.

The victim's sister Diane reported last seeing Connie Sue on Jan. 3 at 2 a.m. at their Peck Street home. Connie Sue had been out the evening before with her boyfriend, Danny Greenberg, and they had gone to a party at one of Danny's friends. Danny had been living with Connie Sue and her sister, but moved out recently and was now living with a friend. He and Connie Sue were experiencing problems in their relationship and at the party they had an argument.

Danny said, "Connie Sue, maybe we should give each other some space and date other people." She had suspicions that Danny was already seeing other girls. "I don't want to see other guys; I want us to be alright."

Danny said, "Let's give it some time."

Perhaps looking for sympathy, Connie Sue stormed into the bathroom and cut her wrist.

The wounds were only superficial and Danny took her home. "What is the matter with you?" Danny demanded. "I don't know," Connie Sue responded. "I need to make some adjustments in my life, and get my priorities straight."

Back at the Peck Street address, the arguing continued. Connie Sue said she was going for a walk and left the house. She never returned home. Diane Willets became concerned that her sister may have met with foul play so she notified the police that her sister was missing.

Family members said Connie Sue was planning to attend airline school and become a flight attendant. She was a good student in high school and had a desire to travel. She was loved by all who knew her; a daughter, a sister, an aunt, and a friend to everyone. Connie Sue's mother had a heart attack when told of her youngest child's fate. She survived the heart attack but died before Connie Sue's killers were found. She went to her grave with many questions and no answers.

At the time of Connie Sue Thompson's death she was a confused, unhappy young woman who met with tragedy. Many young people face these same problems in their lives, but they usually come to their senses and go on to a happy life. Connie Sue Thompson never got this second chance.

Victim – Connie Sue Thompson

Chapter 5
Cheryl Bartlett and Arnold Coates

Twenty-one-year old Arnold Coates, a hard-working and respectable young man, worked in the meat department of the Kroger grocery store in south Toledo. After working the night shift, he left work on the early morning of Jan. 27, 1981.

As Arnold left the store at 12:30, he was met by his 18-year-old fiancée, Cheryl Bartlett, who had walked to the store to meet him. Cheryl had been waiting at their nearby apartment on Segur Avenue for Arnold to get off work.

Cheryl and Arnold, known to his friends as "Bud," lived together with their 15-month-old son, Erik, along with Bud's brother, Don, who was staying with them at the time.

Bud had always told Cheryl not to walk around the neighborhood at night by herself, but on this night she decided to walk to Kroger to meet Bud. She left their son with Don.

Cheryl met Bud at the store and the couple headed for home. The sky was cloudy and the cold wind reddened their faces as they held hands in an attempt to warm each other. As they walked toward home they were approached by a tall black man with short hair, mustache, and a beard. The man was wearing a green Army field jacket.

The man walked past them, then turned around suddenly and

pointed a small 22-caliber revolver at them. The would-be-robber demanded Arnold's wallet. Arnold had put his hands in the air, but the man told him to put them down and act normal. Arnold only had two $1.00 bills in his wallet, and he prayed the robber would not become upset with him for having $2.

The robber was wearing a stocking cap, which he took off and put on Arnold's head, pulling it down over his eyes so he couldn't see. The robber then had Cheryl take Arnold by the arm while he led them both down the street. They were taken to a nearby alley, where they heard a vehicle with a loud muffler. The vehicle stopped near the corner of the alley.

Out of the darkness, another robber appeared and he and the other man talked. The second robber took off his knit cap and placed it on Cheryl's head, pulling it down over her eyes. They were then led back down the alley. They were taken to a garage to the rear of a house on Segur. The garage was dark and cold.

Once inside the garage, Arnold was made to lean against the wall of the garage with his hands clasped behind his back. He was told that if he didn't cooperate he would be shot. They asked Arnold if he had any valuables and when he did not answer he was searched. They took his watch. The robber who had first approached Cheryl and Arnold appeared to be in charge, while the other robber appeared to be slow-minded and a follower.

The second robber said, "I have a knife and will cut you if you don't do as we say." Arnold never saw the second robber because he had the cap pulled down over his eyes, but Cheryl saw both robbers. When they weren't looking she pushed the knit cap up enough so that she could see them. She decided if they were going to kill her she was at least going to look her murderers in the eye.

The couple's worst fears were realized when Cheryl was told to drop her slacks and bend over. Cheryl told the robbers, "I have some rings on and if you don't hurt us and let us go, I will give you my rings." The robbers removed her rings, a white-gold wedding set with three stones, one pink, one yellow, and one green. Even though Cheryl and Arnold were not yet married, Arnold had given her the rings because they were living together as man and wife.

The robbers also removed Cheryl's gold quartz watch with a black face.

The robber with the gun again instructed Cheryl to drop her slacks and bend over.

Arnold was told that if he tried to help Cheryl or resist he would be shot.

Cheryl was told that if she did not cooperate they both would be shot.

After Cheryl cooperated by pulling her slacks and panties down, the robber said, "This is not going to get it." He told her to remove her pants and to lie on the floor of the garage. He then raped her while the other robber held the gun on Arnold. When the first robber was finished the second robber took his turn. After the assaults, Cheryl was made to redress. Cheryl and Arnold were told to hug one another tightly and they would not be harmed.

As Cheryl hugged Arnold and prayed the robbers would leave without killing them, they heard one of them say, "You can now call us pretty niggers if you like, because we are going." As the robbers-rapists fled toward the garage door a shot rang out and Cheryl went limp in Arnold's arms. After Cheryl was shot in the back the would-be killer returned and removed the stocking caps from their heads.

The gunman stared at them when he realized that only Cheryl had sustained the force of the bullet ripping into her back and stomach.

The would-be killer had a look of surprise and fear on his face when he realized Arnold had not felt the bullet piercing his body. Apparently, the gunman only had one bullet in his gun and this is why he made them hug each other tightly. He must have felt that the one bullet would go through Cheryl and into Arnold Coates, killing them both.

When the shooter realized only Cheryl had been wounded he ran.

Arnold and Cheryl managed to struggle to the back door of a home near the garage. Cheryl was so traumatized she didn't even realize she had been shot.

After frantically pounding on the door, a man came to their aid and the Life Squad and police were summoned.

Cheryl was rushed to Medical College Hospital where surgery

was performed and the bullet removed from her stomach. She has had many surgeries and physical problems ever since. Cheryl has never recovered from her emotional and physical injuries, and probably never will.

The bullet taken from Cheryl's body was sent to the crime laboratory for testing and found to be from a Rohm .22-caliber pistol. She and Arnold have never forgotten this terrifying experience, nor have they gotten over the lasting impact of the treatment they endured at the hands of two predators. At the time there was no way to know that they had escaped with their lives from two evil serial killers who had killed in the past – and who would kill again. They were among the few lucky ones who would survive their encounter with these twisted human hunters.

Victims Arnold Coates – Cheryl Bartlett & their son Eric

Chapter 6
Dawn Renay Backes

P retty, vivacious Dawn Backes, 12, looked much older than her young years. Tall, with silky, dark brown hair, brown eyes, and pleasant smile, she could have been mistaken for a high school girl. Dawn was bright, full of life and well liked by her friends. She lived happily with her mother and stepfather, Sharon and Loren Wright, near the University of Toledo.

Sharon Wright loved her only child and they were very close. She did not like being away from Dawn and when they were apart she called and checked on her often.

On Saturday, Feb. 21, 1981, Dawn's parents planned to visit Loren's employer and friend, Edward Baggs, and his wife. While they were away they agreed that Dawn could visit with some of her friends at a local kid' hangout, "Fat Daril's," on Secor Road. Fat Darils sold pizza and had game machines that kids played for entertainment.

The noises coming from the machines, along with the flashing colorful lights, made it a fun place to be. It was located in a strip mall three miles from Dawn's home. Many parents would drop their children off there with a prearranged time to pick them up, or they would get a ride home with a friend.

Fat Daril's was not known as a trouble spot, but the owner employed an off-duty policeman on the weekends to monitor the activities of the kids. There was an off-duty officer working on this Saturday night when Dawn would come up missing.

Loren Wright took his stepdaughter to Fat Darils this Saturday at about 7:15 p.m., stopping first at Dawn's friend's' homes to pick them up. The friends were Sara Wise, 12, and Dorothy Dreslinski, 15.

Mr. Wright was told that all the girls would be given a ride home by the parents of their other friend, Peggy.

Loren gave Dawn the telephone number of his employer's home with explicit instructions to be home by 10:30.

Dawn was happy to be with her friends and felt excited that she had been given the responsibility of being on her own for a few hours. She was wearing a bright yellow blouse, blue jeans, white tennis shoes, and a jacket vest.

It was after 10 p.m. when Dawn, Sara, and Dorothy started looking for Peggy to get their ride home as planned. They discovered that Peggy had left with someone else and had called her father telling him she had a ride home and did not need him to come for them. This caused Dawn discomfort because she had lost the piece of paper with the telephone number her stepfather had given her to call.

As it got later and later, Dawn started to panic because she knew her mother would be furious. Dawn and her friends kept searching for another ride but could find no one to take them home. It was just a little after midnight when the three decided to walk home. As they passed through the nearby McDonald's parking lot, they saw a boy known to them by the name of John.

John was 16 and was driving his mother's car. He had a friend with him named Chris and when the girls asked John to drive them home he replied that he couldn't because he had promised his mother he would not give anyone else a ride in her car. The exact time of 12:03 a.m. was later determined because John remembered looking at a nearby bank clock while talking to the girls.

The girls continued to walk and when they reached the intersection of Central and Secor they parted ways. Sara and Dorothy turned onto Central heading east toward their homes, while Dawn continued South on Secor toward her home.

Dawn's mother, Sharon, started calling her daughter around 11 p.m. to make sure she had gotten home safely. At first she got no answer, but later, while making other attempts, she received a busy signal and felt that Dawn had arrived home and was talking on the telephone. It was later discovered that she and Dawn's friend, Dorothy, had been calling at the same times, explaining the busy signal.

When Sharon finally got through and received no answer, she started to worry. After several more calls, the couple drove home, finding the house uncomfortably quiet.

Sharon called Sara and Dorothy and was told how they had parted company. Dorothy had also called Dawn's home several times after she got home but also received no answer. Sharon called all of Dawn's friends but no one had seen or heard from her.

Dawn was last seen walking near the university, east on Bancroft Street, by two witnesses later interviewed by police. When they heard the young girl was missing they called police and described seeing a girl matching Dawn's description and wearing the same clothing Dawn had on that night. They saw her at 12:15 a.m. on Bancroft near the University of Toledo campus.

They said she was walking east on the north side of the street and was crossing to the south side. Dawn was walking fast because she was late and feared her mother may have been calling her at home to make sure she was there. She was only a few blocks from her house when she vanished.

Sharon called the police and made a missing person report, explaining that Dawn had never disobeyed her in the past and had always come home on time.

Sharon knew something terrible had happened.

Police contacted friends of Dawn but no one had seen her since Sara and Dorothy left her at the corner.

Toledo police put out a broadcast of the missing 12-year-old and checked all the local hospitals. All her friends and relatives were interviewed but no one had seen or heard from her.

Her mother stared at Dawn's empty room. She felt guilt, like all parents would. She couldn't sleep; she cried and prayed for her little girl's safety.

Police interviewed Dawn's friends and the people who were known to have been at Fat Daril's on the night of her disappearance. They were told she had been there and she was seen both inside the establishment and also outside in the parking lot. No one saw anything unusual but her close friends indicated she would not have left with a stranger.

Dawn's mother had always told her not to go into the parking lot, where kids would hang out sometimes, because Sharon felt she would be safe inside the building. When interviewed, the off-duty policeman at Fat Daril's said he encourages the kids to stay inside because they only become vulnerable when leaving the building to hang out with the kids in the parking lot. Most of the kids felt what happened to Dawn had nothing to do with Fat Darils and said that what happened to Dawn could happen to anyone, anywhere.

Four days went by with no sign of Dawn Backes. On Wednesday, Feb. 25, at 8 p.m., police received an anonymous telephone call stating there was a dead body in the basement of the abandoned State Theater on Collingwood Boulevard. The body would later be determined to be that of Dawn Backes, and her death would be ruled a homicide.

The caller first refused to give his name because he said he did not want to become involved. Later, this man and another came forward and gave a full account of their findings. They said that after thinking about it they decided the only right thing to do was to come forward and identify themselves.

Both men were scrutinized and cleared of any criminal involvement. Before they were cleared, they were interviewed separately, their homes were searched for evidence that might involve them in the homicide, and both were given polygraph examinations. No evidence was found in their homes, both passed the polygraph examination, and they answered all questions. The men said they had been searching the abandoned theater for items they could collect; relics, theatrical artifacts, old movie posters, and film memorabilia when they came upon the body.

The State Theater had been abandoned since the 1960s, leaving only wonderful memories of its earlier existence. It was built in early 1927 and opened on Nov. 29, 1927.

The construction cost of the theater was estimated at $500,000 and it was located in the Old West End, where the affluent neighbors were within walking distance.

When the theater opened it presented six vaudeville acts accompanied by an eight-piece pit orchestra. Priority second-run films were an added attraction.

As the years passed the theater experienced a decline in attendance, which the owners blamed on the introduction of television. The movies disappeared and the theater was being used only for special occasions. Several attempts were made to revitalize the theater but by this time the heating, electrical and plumbing deficiencies prohibited this.

In the basement of this once-beautiful Theater now lay the body of a once-beautiful little girl.

After the scavengers found Dawn's body the police were dispatched and the crime scene sealed off. The police found that entry to the theater had been gained through a double set of stage doors located on the side of the building. The doors led to a stairway and to the stage area of the theater, then continued down to the basement and several old dressing rooms.

Dawn's body was found in an open area in front of the dressing rooms.

The Fire Department was requested so its floodlights could be used to light the crime scene. It was so dark that even floodlights did little to illuminate the area.

An adjacent room contained a table where evidence of a struggle could be seen.

The dust on the table had been disturbed and blood spots were found nearby.

The investigators saw that Dawn's head and face had been smashed.

A nearby cinder block, which appeared to have blood on it, was suspected to have been used as the weapon. There was a great deal of blood on the head, face and body of the victim. Blood on the floor around the area where Dawn was found, indicated that she had been murdered there.

The body was lying face down in a pool of blood. Her legs were crossed at the ankles, as if she had been rolled over before the killer or killers left the scene. There were scrape marks on the concrete floor on each side of her head indicating that the cinder block had been thrown at her head more than once. There were abrasions on her hands that indicated she had attempted to fend off her attacker. It was evident that she had fought to survive.

There were blunt-force injuries to the girl's head, face, mouth, left shoulder, and hands. The autopsy found that her vagina was bruised, and perforated. Semen was identified so it appeared she was raped and there were signs that a hard foreign object may have been used to penetrate her. The substantial amount of blood around this area indicated that this assault was committed while the victim was alive.

I was assigned to be the lead investigator and supervisor of the investigation and was to visit the scene the following morning. Although I didn't have the chance to view the crime scene while the victim was still there, I saw it the following morning. Because it was so dark when the body was discovered, a uniformed police crew was stationed at the scene until the investigation could be resumed the next morning. With the aid of the photographs taken the evening before, I was provided with the same conditions as when the body was found.

At the time of this vicious homicide, I had been on the force for 16 years. No case has haunted me more.

During this time of my career, I had the opportunity to have been a detective investigator for all but two of those years. I joined the force on April 2, 1965. With only two years of service I was fortunate to become the youngest police officer in seniority ever to be promoted to the Detective Bureau. From May of 1967 through June of 1976 I was assigned to the Juvenile Bureau as a detective. Within three months I was promoted to the Felony Squad and was assigned serious felony cases involving both juveniles and adults. Those cases involved investigations and arrest for crimes of homicide, robbery, burglary, rape, theft, auto theft, various assaults, drug offenses, vice and prostitution cases.

With the help of others, I was successful in solving cases, including serial cases of those various offenses, and I had a high conviction rate. I enjoy being an investigator, analyzing the facts and evidence of each case, and then putting the pieces together. I find it interesting talking to victims, witnesses and suspects and coaxing confessions from the suspects, then making a solid case to ensure a conviction.

With the assistance of good police officers, witnesses, and victims, I have assisted in making thousands of felony arrests, many of which involved high-profile cases in the city. I loved the work and enjoyed the many hours I have worked in solving cases.

One of my beliefs – and it kept me working hard – is that all citizens have the right to be safe in their homes and on the street.

In July of 1976 I was promoted to sergeant and I have worked and supervised in almost all areas of the Toledo Police Detective Bureau. I have worked in and supervised the Scientific Investigation Unit. I have worked and supervised the Homicide, Burglary, Robbery, Rape, Auto Theft, and Theft squads. I have also worked in the internal affairs section.

At the time of the Dawn Backes homicide, I was the relief sergeant and investigator.

The morning after Dawn Backes was found in the State Theater, I was assigned by the Detective Bureau Section Commander, Deputy Chief Raymond Vetter, to head a task force on this homicide. This was definitely a high-profile case and the news media was on top of it from the night the young victim was reported missing.

The members of our task force were all seasoned detectives. Daniel Foster was assigned to the Personal Assault Unit (Sex Squad) and had a great deal of experience investigating rapes and other sexual assaults. Arthur Marx was a robbery/homicide investigator and had many homicide investigations under his belt. William Adams was a Juvenile Bureau investigator and was successful with working missing person's investigations as well as other serious cases.

My task force was also assisted by two other experienced

investigators, Thomas Ross and Charles Perdeau. Perdeau was a gentle man who had a calming effect while interviewing witnesses. Ross was assigned to the Homicide Squad and had worked on many homicides in the past. All these investigators were highly trained and skilled officers.

I was proud to have these exemplary investigators working with me and I knew I could trust their judgment and work. When you work serious investigations you have to rely on and trust the work ethic of the men beside you.

The task force went over every inch of the theater in search of additional evidence and leads in Dawn's murder.

There were signs that the building had been vandalized, used by loiterers, and picked over by scavengers. I felt strongly that whoever murdered Dawn had been in the theater before and was familiar with the building. To take someone into this dark building at night, where visibility was almost zero, would have taken someone who was very familiar with the internal structure of the theater.

The reconstruction of this crime scene brought tears to my eyes and agony to my heart because of what Dawn must have endured. This was the last curtain call for the State Theater and for young Dawn Backes. The State Theater remained vacant until being torn down on Dec. 16, 1994.

The task force proceeded to the coroner's office and reviewed the autopsy. We examined and discussed the cause of death and evaluated all the evidence. In the months to follow, the task force interviewed well over 100 people and several potential suspects. We brought past rapists in for interrogations and gave polygraphs to potential suspects, including friends and relatives of Dawn.

Crime scene technology turned up very little evidence and, again, there were no latent fingerprints of value. It appeared that whoever committed the crime wore gloves and was careful not to leave trails that would lead to discovery.

The task force's leads were running out and no new ones were being developed. Numerous telephone tips had been received and were checked out before Deputy Chief Vetter reassigned all the members of the task force, with the exception of me and Detective

Adams of the Missing Persons Unit. Unfortunately, crime doesn't stand still in the city just because investigators are working on a high-profile case.

To assist in this investigation, donations for a reward were received from friends, relatives, business organizations and concerned citizens. The total reward money eventually totaled $10,475. I hoped this was an isolated case – but I knew by my many years of experience that it wasn't. There are mitigating circumstances to some antisocial and criminal behavior ... and then there are those who are just plain evil.

I am the type of person who not only wants to solve crime, but I want to know why the person committed the crime. By knowing how society's enemies think, I feel I can better understand them, enhancing my capabilities to make cases.

I also promised myself – and the memory of Dawn Backes – that I would never give up looking for the killer or killers. My nightmares of what happened to this little girl have never ended – and probably never will, until the day I die.

Victim – Dawn Backes

Victim – Dawn Backes holding her dog

State Theater when in operation

Abandoned State Theater where murder victim Dawn Backes was found.

Chapter 7

Denise Siotkowski and
Scott Moulton

Oregon, Ohio is a small city on the outskirts of Toledo in Lucas County. Oregon has a fine police department but because of its size it relies on Toledo to give technical assistance during major crime investigations. Oregon didn't have its own crime laboratory or crime scene technicians. Its police department calls upon the Toledo Police Division's Crime Laboratory and Scientific Investigation Unit to assist from time to time.

On Friday, April 3, 1981, at 9:15 a.m., Pauline Decant, manager of the Fountain Circle Apartments on Navarre Avenue in Oregon, notified Oregon police of a suspicious car. The car, a tan and dark brown Oldsmobile, bearing Ohio tags, had been parked in a carport at the apartment building for several days.

The car did not belong to the person assigned to that carport. Decant had been notified by a tenant, William Callaghan, who reported seeing a black man exiting the car on the passenger side. He witnessed this from his apartment window on Friday, March 27, in the early evening. Over the next few days he noticed that the strange car was still parked in carport No. 8.

48

The Oregon Police Department dispatcher immediately recognized the description and license plate number as that of a car belonging to a missing person, Denise Siotkowski. She had been reported missing on March 30 by her sister, Elaine Clary. She was reported missing along with a friend named Scott Moulton – both were last seen together when they left the Centre Market in Oregon after work on March 27, at 5:30 p.m.

Denise Siotkowski was 21, single and living with her mother in north Toledo. Scott Moulton was also 21 and single; he had also been reported missing by his father, Darrell Moulton.

Denise and Scott were employed with the Centre Market Food Store on Navarre Avenue in Oregon.

Scott was an assistant store manager and had been with the company several years. The store manager described him as a hard worker and excellent employee. He described Denise as dependable, a good worker and excellent with regard to customer relations and service. She was a cashier and had been so since 1976. All the other employees were fond of Scott and Denise and on occasion socialized with them after work.

Employees who worked for Scott at the store said he was a boss you could talk and kid with. When you did something wrong Scott didn't jump all over you, he would explain what you did wrong and try to help you improve.

Fellow employees remarked that Denise was so friendly; many regular customers would wait in her long checkout line while other lines were much shorter, just because they liked talking with her.

Interviews by Oregon detectives found that Denise and Scott were becoming interested in one another, even though both were dating other people on a steady basis. They had taken an interest in each other over the last few months.

It was payday that Friday and Scott and Denise had received their paychecks before leaving together. A check of their time cards indicated that Denise and Scott punched out at 5:27 p.m. Apparently, Scott rode with Denise because his car was later found in the Centre Market parking lot.

Scott and Denise had been invited by other Centre employees to

49

meet them at a local meeting place, Luda's Restaurant. They indicated they would stop by but never arrived. They were, however, seen around 6 p.m. at Connie Barron's Mexican Restaurant. A waitress there said Scott had four Michelob beers and Denise had two strawberry margaritas. They talked, laughed, and seemed to be enjoying themselves while eating cheese chips, bean Tostitos, and tacos.

The waitress said Scott and Denise stayed for about two hours, and then they left together. This would be the last time the two young people would be seen alive.

A week went by while relatives and friends searched frantically for them. Then, the morning of April 3, the Fountain Circle manager, Pauline Decant, made the call to Oregon Police that friends and family were dreadfully afraid would come. Denise's car had been found, backed into carport No. 8.

Oregon police responded to Fountain Circle and went to the car. The registration indeed came back to Denise Siotkowski. The officers tried the car doors, which were locked. They called Denise's mother who said Denise's boyfriend, Gary Ayers, had an extra set of keys to Denise's car. Gary was called and he brought the extra set of keys to the police station. The keys were taken to the scene and Gary and his mother followed in their car. They stayed in their car while the police unlocked the trunk.

Inside were the bodies of Denise and Scott. The crime scene was sealed off and the coroner's office, the Crime Laboratory, and Scientific Investigation Unit, were summoned. Coroner's investigator Tim Fish, Laboratory technician John Alexander, crime scene investigator Edwin Marok, and I arrived to assist with the investigation of the crime scene.

When I arrived on the scene, technicians Alexander and Marok were already working with Oregon detectives Daniel Peacock and Michael Belcik.

Scott's body was nearest the trunk opening and his back was facing out. Denise's body was beneath him and facing Scott's. His arms and hands were positioned behind his back and several powder burns could be seen on the back of his jacket. Upon further scrutiny it was found that the couple had been shot multiple times. It appeared they were killed while in the trunk.

Scott's wallet was found in his left front jacket pocket and all of his credit cards and personal papers were there. The only thing missing was the money he had after cashing his check, probably around $100.

Denise's purse, wallet, credit cards and other personal effects were found under her left arm. The only thing missing was the money from her paycheck. Missing from Denise's car console was a Clarion radio/cassette tape player combination stereo. The investigators later got the model and serial numbers so they could be identified if found. The numbers were later put into the police computer system network in hopes that someone would get caught with the stereo.

I wanted to see if these murders might be similar to the homicide of Thomas Gordon and the attempted murder and rape of his girlfriend, Sandra Podgorski. The crimes appeared similar, but I didn't know if they were murdered by the same perpetrators. Yet even though Dawn Backes wasn't in a car when she was abducted, I had a hunch that all these crimes could have been committed by the same killers.

The Toledo area has its share of homicides, but most are domestic-or robbery-related. It would be highly unusual to have more than one serial killer capable of carrying out such vicious slayings in the same general area.

Gordon and Podgorski were abducted in Gordon's car 10 months earlier, but there were a lot of similarities to this latest case. The victims were robbed, the female raped, and all but Podgorski were violently murdered. The killers in that case left her for dead. Two black men were involved in the assaults on Gordon and Podgorski, and a black man had been seen leaving the passenger's side of Siotkowski's car.

Dawn Backes was also violently murdered after being abducted and raped. After her murder, I started paying closer attention to the violent crimes coming in, and I also began looking at the crimes that had occurred in the past year or two.

The coroner ruled the death of Scott Moulton due to homicide and reported that he had been shot three times in the head and one time in the left side of the back. He ruled that Denise Siotkowski's death was a homicide and stated she had been shot five times in the head. Both were shot at close range.

After the autopsies and the examination of the bullets taken from the bodies, it was determined that Scott and Denise were shot with a .22-caliber pistol. Two months earlier, Cheryl Bartlett and Arnold Coates had been abducted from the street and taken to a garage by two black men. Cheryl was raped then made to hug her boyfriend while being shot in the back with a .22.

None of the bullets were of sufficient ballistic value to be compared with any handgun to a scientific certainty. The make and caliber of the weapons could be determined, but because the bullets were fragmented, there were insufficient ballistic characteristics to match the bullets that killed and wounded these victims with a particular gun.

Cheryl Bartlett, Scott Moulton, and Denise Siotkowski were all shot with the same type of .22-caliber with eight lands and grooves, right-hand twist, and rifling characteristics consistent with RG Industries revolvers. All the rape victims in these cases were made to redress after the rapes – as if the killer or killers may have been trying to cover up the rapes.

Oregon detectives interviewed many witnesses, friends, relatives, and suspects, but they were unable to develop any solid leads. As in the cases of the other homicides and rapes, the leads went cold.

Victim – Denise Siotkowski

Victim – Scott Moulton

Siotkowski's car parked in carport with victims bodies in trunk.

Victim Siotkowski's car at Fountain Circle Apartments in Oregon, Ohio

Chapter 8

Janie Fall
The one that got away

Eighteen-year-old Janie Fall lived in the North End with her husband. He was in the Air National Guard and she supplemented their income by working at Kentucky Fried Chicken on Stickney Avenue.

Her husband was scheduled for an assignment in Greenland and she was trying to work out a way she could travel and be with him. They were newlyweds and they didn't want to be apart, but a military tour in Greenland doesn't make for the best of circumstances.

On the evening of June 22, 1981, Janie had to work at Kentucky Fried Chicken and was not due to get off work until 11:30 p.m. Her husband had promised to pick her up after work, but as she prepared to leave for the evening, he still had not arrived. She waited for awhile, and then decided to walk home. She told her friends at work to watch for her husband and, if he showed up, to tell him that she had started walking home. She hoped he would catch up with her.

It was a warm comfortable night and she really didn't mind the walk. She walked briskly down Stickney to Central Avenue, and then turned left onto Central. She was happy and felt good now that she was off work.

The stars were shining and the full moon lit up the sky. It was a lovely night. As she walked she could sense the quiet of the night and the whisper of the soft wind as it blew through her hair. As Janie turned onto Central she saw a beat-up old dark green and white pickup truck, driven by a black man, slowly pass by her. She didn't think much of it and kept walking.

Janie walked for a couple of blocks and then saw the same truck passing her again. She continued walking but was getting a little uneasy, so she picked up her pace. As she approached an overpass the truck passed a third time. She went around a curve in the road, toward Columbus street, near home.

Janie wondered where the pickup truck had gone. Suddenly, she heard the sound of a chain-link fence being rattled. She looked across the street and saw the black man she had seen in the pickup emerging from a hole in the fence. She described him as 35 to 40, 5 feet, 10 inches tall, 175 pounds, with a mustache and goatee, a small amount of gray in his hair and wearing blue faded jeans, a green, white and gray flannel shirt, and a baseball cap, possibly gray in color.

The man ran across the street to where she was walking and grabbed her. She screamed but her attacker told her to shut up. He was dragging her toward the hole in the fence but she struggled frantically and kept screaming. Her abductor struck her several times while dragging her toward the opening in the fence.

Janie had been carrying a small bag of food for her husband, and it was the only thing she had to defend herself with.

She started hitting the abductor with the bag of food in an attempt to free herself. Janie finally broke free, but as she started to run, her assailant tackled her by the ankles. He dragged her down a hill toward the fence. During the struggle the assailant took hold of her blouse and tried to rip it off. His hand had a grip on her employee badge along with her blouse but, the badge came off and he lost his grip.

The man fell about six feet down the hill and Janie ran for her life.

She ran until she felt her lungs would explode. She reached a house on Columbus Street where a lady came to the door and took her inside. The police and an ambulance were summoned and upon their arrival Janie was taken to St. Vincent Hospital.

A witness standing at the corner saw the victim running and screaming. He saw her run up to the house and approached to see what was wrong. When Janie told him what the assailant tried to do, the witness went searching for him. He met up with another man and together they spotted the assailant and chased him down the railroad tracks. There, they saw the abductor enter his pickup truck and flee.

At the hospital, Janie was observed to have a large bump on her forehead and bruises on the head and body.

Toledo Police Detective Robert Oberdorf was assigned to do the preliminary investigation. He had the badge torn from Janie's blouse fingerprinted but there were no prints of value found. He put out a police broadcast describing the abductor and his pickup truck, but no leads were developed.

Oberdorf searched the entire North End looking for the pickup and the assailant without success.

Janie had gotten a good look at her attacker and his truck so investigators felt she would be able to make identification if and when the assailant and the truck were located. When Detective Oberdorf and I later reviewed this case we noted that the abductor and his truck matched the description in the Thomas Gordon and Sandra Podgorski case.

As for Janie, despite her harrowing experience, she could count herself one of the lucky few who had escaped from one of the killers who stalked free in Toledo.

Chapter 9

Charles Hackenberg and
Laurie Specht
My brother saved us

It was just after midnight on Thursday, July 23, 1981, and the softball game was over. Charles Hackenberg, 20, was heading back from his game in nearby Erie, Michigan, driving his Chevrolet Nova. Both he and his 19-year-old girlfriend, Laurie Specht, were athletic – she, too, played softball, but for a different team. She had a game at Detwiler Park in Toledo at the same time as Charles game.

On the way home, Charles decided he would stop by Laurie's house and visit for awhile. He arrived at her home in North Toledo around 1 a.m. He parked his car in front of Laurie's home and walked to the door.

Upon checking with her brother, John Specht, he found Laurie had not yet returned home from playing softball. John was with his brothers and they had a friend over, so Charles decided to wait in his car for Laurie to come home.

After the game, Laurie caught a ride with her softball coach. Along with the rest of her team she stopped at Johnny's Bar on the way home to have a drink.

It was a lovely summer night, so Charles rolled down his driver's side window and enjoyed the cool night air coming through the window. He had almost fallen asleep when he heard a car door shut. He looked up and was happy to see Laurie coming toward him.

Laurie got in on the passenger side, hurrying to be embraced while they said their hellos and asked about each others game. While talking, a shadow appeared on the driver's side of the car.

They saw a black man wearing a tan ski mask and holding a pistol. The man appeared to be in his 20s, about 6 feet tall. He was wearing plaid pants and a dark shirt.

The robber ordered Charles to give him his wallet and Charles told him he didn't have one. Laurie told the robber she had a purse and would give that to him. The gunman said he didn't want her purse and yelled at Charles, "Move over, motherfucker!"

Before the robber could force his way into the car, Laurie's brother John walked out onto their front porch and looked in their direction. The robber lifted his ski mask and looked them right in the face, demanding to know who was on the front porch. Both replied that the man was Laurie's brother and that he'd better leave because there were others who would come to their rescue.

The robber said, "I believe you, man," and ran.

"Who was that," John asked. They told him what had happened and they all went into the house. Inside, they told Laurie's other brothers, Albert, 21, Larry, 19, and a friend Manuel, 18, what had occurred. John got his two dogs and he and the other men went looking for the robber.

They had no luck so they returned to the house and called the police. Laurie hugged her brother and said, "Thank God you came out and saved us or we may have been murdered."

At this time we couldn't know if this was one of the killers who had committed the other vicious crimes, but I looked at it as a possibility. The robber was black, he approached Laurie and Charles while they were talking in Charles' car late at night, and he had a gun. He made it clear that he intended more than robbery when he refused Laurie's purse and tried to force his way into the car.

As before, we combed the area for possible witnesses, but the trail again went cold. If Laurie's brother had not walked out onto the porch just as the robber was forcing his way into Charles' car, they could have been abducted like the other victims.

Chapter 10

Stacey Balonek and Daryl Cole

Daryl Cole and Stacey Balonek, both 21, had been introduced to each other by Stacey's brother-in-law, Kenneth Mikolajczyk. Kenneth was married to Stacey's sister, Cynthia. Both Kenneth and Daryl worked at the Centre Market – the same grocery chain where Denise Siotkowski and Scott Moulton worked. Four months earlier, they were murdered a few hours after leaving work. Kenneth first met Daryl while playing racquetball at Supreme Courts. People from the various Centre Markets would meet there occasionally and play. It was a good way to get to know one another while having fun and exercising.

Stacey and Daryl hit it off right away and started dating regularly. Stacey was employed at Rink's Bargain City Store in north Toledo and spent most of her time in shoe sales. Recently, she had been filling in at the south end store as a department manager.

Stacey was a tall, pretty young woman with long brown hair. She lived with her parents Stanley and Muriel Balonek in north Toledo. After graduating from Woodward High School, she began working to earn money so she could train for a career as a respiratory therapist.

Daryl Cole lived with his parents, James and Sally Cole, in Maumee, Ohio, a small city southwest of Toledo. He was working at

Centre Market to earn money for college. Daryl was attending the University of Toledo Community College and wanted to become a police officer. He was a 6-foot, 190-pounder with a muscular build.

Stacey was on the mend from breaking up with her former fiancé when she was introduced to Daryl by her brother-in-law. Even though Stacey and Daryl had only been dating for less than a year, they were getting serious and discussing marriage.

August 1, 1981, was a Saturday, and plans had been made for Stacey and Daryl to go out to dinner with Kenneth, Cynthia, and their two sons. They were to meet at Stacey's house at 6:30 p.m. then, go to the Red Lobster Restaurant.

Kenneth drove Cynthia and their two boys to the Baloneks' home and met with Daryl and Stacey. They left the Baloneks' at 7 p.m. in separate cars.

Daryl drove his Pontiac Grand Prix two-door sedan, with a light tan landau roof. The car was neat: It had chrome wheels, bucket seats, a console shift, and an AM/FM stereo-cassette player. Daryl was proud of his car and kept it exceptionally clean. He felt proud when he drove his car and even prouder when his friends took notice.

Both cars pulled up to the Red Lobster at 7:20 p.m. They ate and talked, leaving the restaurant at 8:30 p.m. They agreed to stop by the apartment of Stacey and Cynthia's brother, Mitchell Balonek. They visited with Mitchell and watched a movie on television until 11 p.m. It was a miserably hot August night. Mitchell's home didn't have air conditioning, so they decided to go to Kenny and Cindy's house, in the far north end of the city.

While at Kenneth and Cynthia's, the group played the game Aggravation, with the women matched up against the men. They played several games when Stacey said she didn't feel well and went upstairs. Soon after, Stacey came back down and she and Daryl decided to leave. Kenneth remembered the time they left as being 2 a.m. Sunday, Aug. 2.

Stacey and Daryl never returned home. At 4 p.m. that Sunday, Stacey's parents, Stanley and Muriel Balonek, decided it was time to report them missing. They spoke to Sgt. Jim Heyneman. Heyneman took the Baloneks' report and issued a missing persons alert. He assigned Detective Bill Adams to conduct a search for the missing couple.

A police broadcast was transmitted to police crews and the surrounding police departments. Because of the recent abductions and killings of young couples, a massive search was launched. Not only were the police searching, but the families and friends of the missing couple searched for them, too, all through North Toledo, with no luck.

Neither the couple nor Daryl's car could be located.

Aug. 3 at 8:15 p.m., 19-year-old Charles Hobbs and his girlfriend, 21-year-old Patricia Mikolajczyk, Kenneth's sister, found Daryl's car parked in front of a house a few blocks from where Stacey lived.

Charles parked behind Daryl's car and approached the abandoned vehicle. He tried the driver's side door and found it unlocked. The passenger's side door was locked. There was a strong odor of death coming from the trunk. He looked for the keys so he could open the trunk but there were no keys. He called Stacey's parents, Stanley and Muriel Balonek. They soon arrived and Muriel started to cry.

She pounded on the trunk of the car, sobbing: "I know they are in there!"

The mother's fears would turn out to be true – when detectives forced open the trunk they found the bodies of Stacey and Daryl. It would later be determined that the bodies had been in the trunk since the early morning hours of Aug. 2

The body of Stacey Balonek was nearest the trunk opening, lying on top of the body of Daryl Cole. She was wearing blue jeans and white bikini underpants. The knees of the blue jeans were dirty, as if she had been on her knees in the dirt.

Stacey was bare from the waist up and her shoes were missing, leaving her barefoot. They were a size 8 and the brand was "Love Mates," with the name being written on a pink tag attached to the shoes.

There were signs of heavy trauma to her head. Both of her eyes were blackened and swollen shut. Stacey's teeth and jaw were shattered and her neck appeared broken.

Daryl lay on his back beneath Stacey. He was clad in a pair of blue jean cut-off shorts, a light blue T-shirt, and flip-flop sandals. His head also bore the signs of blunt force trauma.

It was obvious from the injuries that they had been bludgeoned with a heavy object at another location then, placed into the trunk.

The injuries were massive and if they had been murdered in the car or the trunk there would have been blood splattered throughout. The car had heavy amounts of mud, grass and weeds in the wheel wells and undercarriage, indicating it had been in an off road area. This area would most likely be the scene of the murders, but at this point the location was not known.

Daryl, a baseball player, had baseball bats and balls in the trunk. One of the bats was found to have blood on it. It appeared this was the weapon used to murder the couple.

The bodies of Stacey Balonek and Daryl Cole were transported to the County Morgue so the coroner's office could perform the autopsies.

Victim – Stacey Balonek

Victim – Daryl Cole

Chapter 11
Growing Suspicions

"What is wrong with people?" Angeline Kowalski, Rink's Bargain City supervisor, asked. Describing the murdered Stacey Balonek as a hard-working employee who never caused any problems, Kowalski said Stacey was outgoing and had many friends.

Stacey's sister, Cynthia Mikolajczyk, spoke of her younger sister, one of eight children, as being a wonderful sibling who loved life, family and friends.

Stanley Balonek, father of Stacey, was puzzled by the crime. Stacey and Daryl were both good kids, never causing problems for anyone. They were just normal young people with their whole life in front of them, yet now they are gone.

And here I was involved in yet another case that bespoke pure savagery and evil.

During the long hours the other investigators and I spent working this case and the others; I couldn't help but think of the pain and agony suffered by the victims and their loved ones.

"What makes one human being treat another human being this way?" I thought to myself.

During this time I had three children, Kevin, 15; Carey, 13 and

Amy, 11 – my only daughter the same general age as the youngest victim, Dawn Backes. I thought of that little girl and what pain and fear she had endured before death, and then I thought of my little girl and what life would be like if that happened to her.

I knew my mission in life would be protecting the children and people of my community. I knew if these demonic people were not stopped, the streets would not be safe for any of our families.

At the morgue, the autopsies were performed by Dr. Fazekas. Vaginal and rectal swabs were taken from the body of Stacey Balonek and it was determined that she had been raped.

The coroner, Dr. Mignerey, ruled Stacey and Daryl died as a result of multiple blunt force injuries to the head.

It was becoming apparent to me and some of the more experienced detectives that at least four of these multiple homicides - Denise Siotkowski, Scott Moulton, Stacey Balonek, and Daryl Cole - may be related to the same killer or killers.

I believed it went much deeper than that, and I thought there was a very good possibility those homicides and the killing of Thomas Gordon, the attempted homicide and rape of Sandra Podgorski, the murder and rape of Connie Sue Thompson, the attempted homicide and rape of Cheryl Bartlett and aggravated robbery of Arnold Coates, the murder and rape of Dawn Backes, and the assaults on Janie Fall, Charles Hackenberg and Laurie Specht were all related.

Thomas Gordon had been murdered and placed in the trunk of his car while his girlfriend, Sandra Podgorski, was stabbed and raped by two black men, then left for dead. Connie Sue Thompson had been taken off the street, raped and murdered. Cheryl Bartlett and Arnold Coates were abducted off the street by two black men and Cheryl was raped by both men before being shot in the back, surviving her injuries; Dawn Backes was abducted from the street, raped and murdered; Denise Siotkowski and Scott Moulton were abducted in Denise's car, she was raped and both were murdered; Janie Fall was assaulted by a black man late at night while walking home from work, fortunately escaping without serious harm; and Charles Hackenberg and Laurie Specht were assaulted in Charles' car by a black man.

All these incidents had similar aspects, and many of the victims were abducted from and murdered in the same area. Even though there were some differences in the cases, I felt the trail was leading to the same place.

In an attempt to find the crime scene where Daryl Cole and Stacey Balonek were murdered, and to uncover evidence that would lead to solving these homicides, police heightened their efforts. All crews, especially those assigned to the North End, where the latest bodies were discovered, were called into the search for the crime scene. Many of the top detectives were summoned to assist in looking for clues, interviewing witnesses and relatives, and searching for the crime scene. We desperately wanted to find the latest scene in the hope that some trace of evidence would lead to a break in the case. All the officers involved worked hard and diligently as a team with a mission.

Detective James Carnes, a veteran sex unit investigator; James Detrick, an experienced missing persons investigator; William (Bill) Adams, an experienced missing persons and felony investigator; Sam Harris, a vice/metro investigator; homicide investigators Thomas Ross, Arthur Marx, and I began the long and tedious job of attempting to find evidence that would bring someone to justice.

Friends, relatives, fellow employees, and Stacey's past fiancé and neighbors were interviewed. All of the people living in the area where Daryl Cole's car was found, with the bodies in the trunk, were interviewed.

On Aug. 11, police finally got a break in the case. Sgt. Michael Schroeder had some time between his calls and started searching an area where he felt the latest homicides could have occurred. He drove along a dirt service road adjacent to two sets of railroad tracks under the Central Avenue overpass that runs parallel to I- 280 and the N & W tracks. Sgt. Schroeder, as well as Toledo police and officers from surrounding jurisdictions, were diligently trying to come up with clues.

Schroeder stopped his patrol car and got out. He began walking the tracks, looking for any trace of evidence that the homicides may have occurred there. As he walked under the overpass along the wooded, weedy area, he spotted what he believed were the missing sandals of Stacey Balonek. The sandals were within a foot of each other. He checked the sandals and found that indeed they bore the name of Love Mates which matched the identical description of the ones missing from Stacey Balonek. He immediately called the Detective Bureau, and Detective Ross was dispatched to the scene.

Ross arrived with the Toledo Police Crime Lab's Josh Franks. After they arrived, a further search was conducted. They began searching the area, covering both sides of the tracks. They noticed flies around the area of an old discarded rug. Near this rug they found several large patches of dried blood, a tooth and two pieces of bone later found to be from a human jawbone. They also found a woman's gold necklace and several pieces of small cord, which appeared to match that of the pieces found entwined in Stacey's hand when she was found.

On the northeast side of the tracks was more evidence of blood. Franks conducted a preliminary chemical test at the scene, which revealed the find to be indeed human blood.

The tooth and jaw parts appeared to be embedded in the soil. The victims apparently were struck so hard with the baseball bat, found in the trunk of Daryl Cole's car, that the force caused the tooth and jaw fragments to be dislodged and partially embedded in the dirt. Crime scene Technician Larry Mallory arrived on the scene and took photographs of all the area and suspected evidence. He collected it and prepared a crime scene sketch.

The next day, Aug. 12, I took a search party back to the scene, hoping to find more evidence. I set up a command post under the Central Avenue overpass where the evidence had been found.

I organized two search parties. They covered the entire area and beyond. There was no doubt that Schroeder had located the crime scene.

One search team was made up of Sgt. Schroeder, Detective James Carnes, Officer James Merrit , Officer Robert Sweede and Officer Harold Mosley. They were assigned to search the east tracks area. The second team consisted of Sgt. Phillip Wesley, Detective Pat Allen, Detective Bill Adams, Officer Larry Scoble and Officer Oscar Martinez. They searched the west tracks area. The tracks had heavy rust on them and appeared as if they were no longer in use.

Signs of a struggle were found near the railroad tracks. It appeared that one of the victims tried to escape – there were what appeared to be clawing marks in the cinders and gravel at the scene.

The evidence found did not lead directly to an arrest, but investigators were able to build on the suspicion that the killer or killers here had killed Thomas Gordon. The body of Gordon and his badly injured girlfriend, Sandra, were abandoned in his car on McLean Street, which is just above where this crime scene was located. The proximity of these two murder investigations made it appear that the killer lived in this area – or was at least familiar with it.

Investigators interviewed nearby residents. Some residents said that the railroad tracks were a common dumping place but no one saw anything suspicious.

The murders of Scott Moulton, Denise Siotkowski, and Thomas Gordon were very similar to the Balonek and Cole murders because they were abducted at one location, murdered in another place, then brought back to the area they were abducted from. It was becoming obvious that we had at least one serial killer working our city and surrounding areas. It was a frightening thought because we knew he or they would strike again.

By this time, local folks began to worry for themselves. The recent deaths were plastered on the front pages of the newspaper and on television. The victims' families struggled to cope with their loss.

We continued to search for the killers, but we were no closer to an arrest than we were months before. Thousands of dollars in reward money was offered by family and friends of the victims, community groups, the prosecutor's office, and other organizations, but still no new tangible leads developed. Most criminals talk, and sooner or later someone will come forward with what they have heard, but that was not the case during this series of brutal crimes. The serial killers kept silent.

One thing we did know – we were not dealing with first-time offenders.

Toledo Police detectives Bill Adams on the left and Jim Carnes on the right look for evidence at the scene of the Balonek and Cole murders.

Chapter 12

Mark Wiler

The Norfolk & Western railroad freight train crawled noisily down the tracks, returning from its Detroit/ Toledo Shoreline Railroad run. Though it was a clear night, the moon and stars shed very little light. There was little dew on the ground while the late evening air was warm and humid. It was Monday, Aug. 17, 1981, at 11:05 p.m. as the train engineer and his fireman absently gazed out the windows of the locomotive while crossing New York Street heading west, parallel to Joseph Street, in North Toledo.

As the engine led slowly along the tracks, it followed a slight curve to the left. The silhouette of the wooded area to the south could faintly be seen through the darkness. About 150 yards from New York Street, on the right side of the tracks, an object was illuminated by the locomotive's headlights. As they got closer, the engineer and fireman saw a body lying face down, with the head pointing northwest. The body was about 15 feet off the tracks and the person was not moving. The body was far enough away that it could not be seen from New York Street.

The engineer radioed the terminal and Detective Bernard Lamb of the Norfolk & Western Railroad police went to the scene. The train crew reported that they had traveled this same route, in the opposite direction, an hour before but did not see the body.

Lamb notified the Toledo Police dispatcher. He sent Officers Rick Hanus and Al Segura to the scene. Upon arrival they sealed off the area and waited for the on-call homicide detective, Tom Ross, to arrive.

A sergeant and another officer assisted in protecting the crime scene. Crime scene technician Mallory was dispatched and took photographs. Tire tracks were found beyond the stopped police vehicles, indicating another vehicle had been driven to the area where the body lay.

The victim was a white male, mid-to late 30s; 5 feet, 10 inches tall with a stocky build; dishwater blonde, wavy hair; thick mustache; and wearing a long-sleeve, bright-red shirt and tan dress pants without a belt. The man was not wearing shoes nor could any shoes be found. He was lying face down with his head resting on his arms and his feet were close together. Rigor mortis had set in.

Rigor mortis is detected by the stiffness of the body joints and takes about 10 to 12 hours to complete when the temperature is 70 to 75 degrees. Rigor lasts 24 to 36 hours before the body muscles soften. The assistant coroner, Dr. Fazekas, would later rule that this victim died between 2 a.m. and 6 a.m. Monday, Aug. 17.

The right side of the victim's head showed blunt force trauma and there were bruises about the face. Blood was in the victim's hair and covered his head and face. The blood had run down on his clothing to his feet. He had no shoes and his feet were covered with blood and mud. This evidence indicated that the victim was struck about the head while standing.

Technician Mallory photographed the location of the body and surroundings. He made a crime scene sketch and the area where the body was found was marked off so it could be located later. Coroner's Investigator Tim Fish was contacted by telephone and he advised that the body was to be transported to the Lucas County Morgue. The victim's hands were bagged so they could later be examined and fingernail scrapings could be taken. The body was then removed to the morgue by county transport.

The ground where the police cruisers were parked was marked so it would be known exactly where the crime scene started. It was too dark to do a thorough crime scene search, so a police crew was stationed overnight to protect the scene.

The nearest building to the crime scene was the McDonald's Restaurant warehouse on the northeast corner of New York and Joseph. It was learned that there was a guard shanty located there, manned by a guard. In the shanty was a surveillance monitor tied to a parking lot camera. The guard was questioned but said he saw nothing during his rounds of the premises, nor did he view anything suspicious on the camera monitor. He said that the camera was of poor quality and very little could be detected in its images. The lighting was so poor in the parking lot and surrounding area that the camera detected only darkened images.

After first light, technician Mallory returned to further his investigation. While the uniformed policemen continued to protect the scene he started his search for evidence. Detective Ross met Mallory a short time later.

Mallory walked down the left side of the tracks on the well-maintained and freshly graveled service road, back toward where the body was found. Evidence would be fairly easy to locate because the weeds between the tracks and the woods had been recently cut. As he walked, he searched for evidence and took photographs. When he got to the point adjacent to where the body was found, he turned left, heading southwest into the trees. About 10 feet into the woods he found a blood-stained 12-foot piece of white plastic/nylon rope tied to a small tree. Also tied to the tree were a bright red necktie and a white two-wire electrical cord that appeared to be from a small appliance of some kind.

A white swimsuit with a red elastic belt was found at the foot of the tree and it was soaked with blood. It appeared that the victim was tied to this tree then the swimsuit was placed over his head. It further appeared he was then struck on the right side of his head with a blunt object causing heavy bleeding, which saturated the swimsuit.

No blood was found to have been splattered on or around the tree, indicating the swimsuit absorbed most of the blood from the victim's head.

Apparently, the killer left the victim for dead but sometime after he fled the victim managed to free himself from his bonds. It appeared he then crawled or staggered about 72 feet to the other side of the railroad tracks where he was found.

His will to live could not overcome his injuries.

My first thought was, "Is this the latest victim in the series of homicides?" The body of the victim was found less than a mile from where Stacey Balonek and Daryle Cole were murdered. Their deaths had occurred only two weeks before and they had been bludgeoned to death as well.

I felt the urgency to find whoever was responsible.

Soil and foliage samples were taken from the scene and all the evidence was collected. Photographs of the victim and his fingerprints were taken at the morgue in an attempt to determine who he was.

Dr. Fazekas, the assistant coroner, performed the autopsy. It was her opinion, based on the stage of rigor, fixed lividity and the presence of maggots on the victim's face, that death occurred between 2 a.m. and 6 a.m. The cause of death was ruled blunt force injury to the head. No weapon was found.

The hunt was now on to seek the identity of the victim. Missing Persons officers contacted all the area and state police agencies.

They were given the description of the victim in hope that they might get a missing person report that matched. Photographs of the victim were shown to the local police crews in the hope that they might recognize the victim, but there were no identifications.

Finally, police got a break in the case when Detective Charles Perdeau received a telephone call Aug. 19. The call was from Sgt. Fiser of the Ohio Highway Patrol. Fiser said he had just received a call from a David Smith of Flint, Michigan, who was reporting a man missing that matched the description of the Toledo victim. Twenty minutes later, Detective Thomas Staff contacted Smith, an employee at the Buick Division of the GMC Plant in Flint.

Smith and Barbara Anderson were worried about an employee in the plant, Mark Wiler. Smith was a fellow employee and Anderson was Wiler's immediate supervisor. The description of Wiler matched that of the Toledo victim.

They said Wiler had left work Aug. 14 enroute to Columbus to attend a wedding over the weekend. He was driving a white 1980 Buick Regal with a light blue partial vinyl roof, bearing Michigan license plates GMR 356. The car was registered in the name of David Smith, who had allowed Wiler to drive it while buying and paying for it. They were good friends, Smith said.

Both Smith and Anderson became concerned when Wiler did not show up for work on Monday morning. It would have been very unusual for Wiler to miss work, explained Anderson, especially without calling in. She called Wiler's mother, Bettye Wiler, who lived in Columbus. She learned from the mother that Wiler had stayed with friends Pam White and Jim Miller in Columbus, until Aug. 16, at 11:30 p.m., when he left for home.

Mark was a good-hearted soul who would do anything for his friends and family, said his mother, Bettye Wiler. While a former lieutenant in the U.S. Army, he served a tour in Vietnam. Mark graduated from Franklin Heights High School, and he attended Kent State University. He finished his degree in education from Ohio State University.

Since the description of Mark and the description of the clothing he was last seen wearing matched that of the Toledo victim, arrangements were made for David Smith to come to Toledo to identify the body. Mr. Smith indicated he would fly to Toledo in his own airplane. With him was a fellow employee, Al Ball, who also knew Mark well and had come along to assist with the identification.

Detective Staff and Sgt. Ralph Kuyoth picked them up at the airport and drove to the coroner's office. Smith and Ball took a look at the body – it was Mark Wiler.

With the victim identified, a description of his car was broadcast nationally. We hoped that the killer or killers would get caught with the car, or at least evidence would be found when the car was located. A description of what Mark was wearing – clothing, jewelry, watch, shoes, and a description of what he had with him was also broadcast.

On Aug. 17, before the body was found, some of Mark's personal property was discovered by three young boys playing at Chase Park, which is near the area where the body lay.

While the boys, all brothers, were making a tree fort, they found Mark's Social Security card and pilot's certificate. They also found his wallet, but it was empty. A hairdryer without a cord, a belt, and a good amount of clothing, later identified as Mark's, was in the bushes and wooded area behind the park. The missing cord from the hairdryer was later found to have been used to tie Mark to the tree before his death. Lab technicians matched the cord with the hairdryer.

On Aug. 21, Capt. Robert Marti was working the Toledo Police Detective Bureau desk when he received a call from Columbus Detective John Shawkey. He was advised they had located the 1980 Buick Regal belonging to Wiler in an alley. Shawkey said they were keeping the car under surveillance for a while, hoping to catch someone coming back to it. After a few hours the car was towed and secured until it could later be processed for latent fingerprints and evidence.

On Aug. 22, Detective Staff and Sergeant Kuyoth traveled to Columbus to help process the stolen car. After briefing the Columbus officers, all drove to the Franklin County Coroner's Office, where the car was processed.

The car keys were missing and the ignition was locked. The original license plates were on the car. The gas gauge indicated there was a quarter tank of gas left. The dome light cover was missing and the light bulb had been broken. The dome light cover was one of the things found behind Chase Park earlier in the investigation. Apparently the killer or killers had removed the light cover and broke the light bulb so they would not be seen going through Wiler's car.

The car was processed for fingerprints and the items in the car were inventoried. Many fingerprints were located but most were later eliminated as belonging to the victim and his friends. No evidence of value was found.

A serial killer from the Akron area named Thomas Gilbert had been in the Toledo area in July and August. In July he was under investigation by the Monroe, Michigan police for the abduction and murder of a woman leaving a Kroger' store. The Kroger store was located in Lucas County, near Toledo, Ohio, but after the woman was abducted she was taken just over the Michigan/Ohio line, where she was murdered.

Gilbert had fled back to the Akron area, where he abducted, raped and murdered a 19-year-old woman. He also abducted a 14-year-old girl off the street in Akron and raped and murdered her behind a school, abandoning her there. He was convicted for the Akron area murders and is doing life in prison. There was insufficient evidence to convict Gilbert for the murder of the woman taken from the Kroger store.

Thinking Gilbert may have been involved in the Wiler murder I contacted the Akron Police and found that their murders occurred on Aug. 12 and 14, and Gilbert was arrested during the daytime on Aug. 16, in Akron. Mark Wiler was murdered between 2am and 6am on Aug. 17, and since Gilbert was in jail on Aug. 16, he was eliminated as a suspect in the Wiler murder.

After working on the Wiler homicide, reading all the reports from the other investigators, talking to them, viewing the murder scene and park area where most of the victim's property was recovered and analyzing all the evidence, my feelings were stronger than ever that the same killer or killers were responsible for all these murders. Although we had no concrete evidence to identify anyone or to link all or most of the cases to specific killers, the common denominators were strong.

From the statements made by Mark Wiler's friends in Columbus I knew that Mark Wiler left Columbus at 11:30 p.m. on Sunday, Aug. 16. The coroner put the time of death between 2 a.m. and 6 a.m. that Monday. I knew that Mark had purchased a small amount of marijuana while in Columbus and had used most of it. I knew that he would not pick up hitchhikers, so the chances of someone getting to him between Columbus and Toledo were slim.

I theorized that Mark may have stopped in Columbus right after he left his friend's home to buy more marijuana. If so, it was there that he was assaulted and abducted. I further theorized that the killer or killers were from the Toledo area and knew friends or had relatives in Columbus. It appeared Mark was brought to Toledo and murdered in this remote area because the killer was familiar with it.

After robbing and murdering Mark, the killer drove the car to Chase Park and went through his belongings. The dome light cover was removed and the light bulb was broken so the killer would not be detected going through Mark's belongings. The car was then driven back to Columbus where the killer picked up his own car.

The time Mark left Columbus and the time of death was just enough time for the killer to bring Mark to Toledo. Since the other victims, Thomas Gordon and Sandra Podgorski, Janie Fall, Charles Hackenberg and Laurie Specht, Stacey Balonek and Daryl Cole, were all assaulted and or murdered in this same general area, I further theorized that the same killer may have been responsible for all these crimes, and possibly others.

I knew that only time would tell, but I also dreaded the thought that the killer – or killers – were still out there.

Chapter 13

Lorena Zimmerman

On a hot, humid Saturday night, Aug. 29, 1981, 18-year-old Lorena Zimmerman, her 21-year-old sister April Walentowski, and their girlfriends, Teresa Warner, Dawn Meyers, and Debbie Sampson, decided to go to Kip's Night Club in West Toledo for a good time. The club was air-conditioned and they could escape the heat while dancing and socializing.

Teresa's uncle, Jeff Williams, agreed to drive the girls to the club.

Kip's was a popular nightclub where young adults met on the weekends for a little entertainment. Most of the young people who frequented the club were single, and the opportunity for new friends existed.

Lorena was attractive, 5 feet, 4 and 120 pounds, with blue eyes, light brown shoulder-length hair that had recently been bleached to blonde. She was adventurous and had a rose tattoo on her right upper bicep. Her sister, April, had one just like it.

Lorena wore a multi-colored glitter halter top with the suggestive saying across the front: "Yes I do but not with you." She also wore Wrangler blue jeans with a silver thread swirl design on the pockets and the cuffs were rolled up. She liked and wore a lot of costume jewelry.

She carried her Michigan driver's license and $6 in cash in her jean pocket.

Lorena was employed as a clerk for the West Toledo Herald newspaper and she was a strong-headed, independent person.

While at Kip's, Lorena listened to the music and danced with a young man. It was almost midnight when most of the group decided to head for home, leaving Lorena and April at the bar alone. On their outings, the group always left around midnight and, usually, Lorena and April would leave with them, but on this night they decided to linger.

April talked with a young man and, not realizing he was the same man her sister had been dancing with, invited him to her table. When Lorena noticed April with him she became enraged with April and said she was leaving and would walk home. Lorena left carrying a trench coat she had brought along in case it rained. April wasn't worried because Lorena had become upset on other occasions then would return after she cooled off – and all would be well.

Kip's closed at 2 a.m. and Lorena still hadn't returned. April figured she must have gotten a ride with a friend or actually did walk home. When April got home she found that Lorena wasn't there. She thought Lorena might have walked over to her past boyfriend Dean's home – he lived just a short distance away in a trailer, behind the Hungry I Restaurant. Lorena had lived with Dean for awhile but they broke up several months before.

April called their friends but no one knew where Lorena was.

Joe and Mike Foxhuber were adult brothers and both lived in Toledo until Mike and his family moved to Florida. After four months, Mike decided to move back to Toledo, because the job market wasn't as good in Florida.

On Aug. 30, it was almost 4 p.m. when Joe and Mike decided to go fishing. They decided to catch their own bait rather than pay $1.15 a dozen for worms.

Mike suggested they look along the railroad tracks near the 100 block of Westwood Avenue. The closest business in the area was Kripke-Tuschman Industries on Westwood. This area was ideal for worms because there was a lot of old discarded cardboard, wood and other items that worms would lie under. It had been raining earlier and the ground was soft, making conditions excellent for night crawler searching. They had plastic buckets and shovels and started digging for bait.

After collecting a few worms, Mike noticed a discarded piece of old carpet with a tire and piece of plywood on top of it. Mike stepped on the carpet and got an eerie feeling. He described to Joe that it felt like he had stepped on a human leg.

Mike removed the tire and piece of wood. As he pulled back the carpet he saw a face staring back at him and first thought it was a mannequin. But a closer look revealed the dreadful truth. This face belonged to that of a dead woman. They scurried off looking for a telephone to notify police. Joe remembered seeing a man working at the lumber mill near where they drove in. Both of them ran to the building and asked the man if they could use the telephone.

The police responded to the call within minutes. Mike and Joe directed the police to where the body was found.

Police crews guarded the area while detectives and a coroner's investigator were called to the scene. Crime Scene Technician Pete Hodak was there to preserve the evidence. Upon removing the debris covering the body, investigators found a nude female lying on her back with her head toward the railroad tracks. Detectives McDavid McCorvey and Tom Ross, along with Coroner's Investigator Tim Fish, examined the body and surroundings.

The victim was a white female, in her late teens or early 20s with bleached blonde hair; with a rose tattoo on her right bicep. There were no clothes found and rigor had set in the body. The area around the victim's eyes was bruised from apparent trauma to the face and head. There were bruises on her shoulders and neck and it appeared she had been strangled. Fingernail punctures and scratches were observed around the woman's neck, typical of defensive wounds. It appeared the victim had been fighting for her life while attempting to pull the killer's hands from her throat.

The body was located approximately 50 yards northeast of the 100 block of Westwood Avenue, adjacent to the Conrail/Airline junction railroad tracks. Tire tracks were observed near the area of the body and could not be accounted for, so Hodak made plaster moulages of the impressions. In examination of the body, blood could be observed coming from the area of the victim's vagina, indicating she may have been sexually assaulted.

Forensic pathologists Steven and Renate Fazekas performed the autopsy. Through their examination the coroner, Dr. Mignerey, ruled the death a homicide due to strangulation. They also found semen on the vaginal smears, indicating the victim had been sexually assaulted. A set of the woman's fingerprints were taken in an attempt identify her.

Meanwhile, Detective William Knapp of the Robbery/Homicide Squad received a telephone call from his wife, Peggy Knapp, a licensed practical nurse in the Mercy Hospital Emergency Room. Peggy advised her husband that she had received a telephone call from Arline Zimmerman, who wanted to know if her daughter, Lorena, had been admitted to the hospital.

Arline Zimmerman said her daughter had been missing for 18 hours and she was checking the hospitals to see if her daughter had met with an accident of some sort. She provided Knapp with a description of her daughter, and the description met the description of the murder victim. Lorena's father, Ralph, was directed to the Lucas County Morgue at 9:15 p.m. and he identified the body as that of his daughter.

I tracked down Lorena's former boyfriend, Dean Shelton, because the victim's sister, April, believed her sister might have walked to his home for a ride. April said Dean lived near Kip's and she thought Lorena might have gone there.

I questioned Dean, who said he and Lorena were more friends than lovers. Lorena had stayed at his mobile home on and off. They dated until July when Dean started seeing his old girlfriend Kimberly. Dean said that the last time he saw Lorena was around the middle of July.

Dean insisted that Lorena did not come to his home on Sunday morning, and he provided an alibi. The alibi was verified and Dean agreed to submit to a polygraph examination.

Dean passed the examination and was no longer considered a suspect.

There were similarities between Zimmerman's homicide and that of Connie Sue Thompson, who was strangled and stabbed to death on Jan. 4. Connie Sue had been abducted, taken to a secluded area, raped, and killed, then left under Bancroft Street in a culvert. Both of the victims were young white females.

Investigators could not rule out that the killer or killers were the same. Nor could we say otherwise.

But, I found it hard to believe that we could have that many different cold-blooded, sadistic killers out there targeting only young white people, and I believed this latest rape and murder could be related to the others.

The news media jumped on the murders and the pressures to make an arrest grew.

I punished myself with the solemn thoughts that someone had again outsmarted us – and was free to strike again.

Victim – Lorena Zimmerman

Scene of murder in South Toledo

Chapter 14

Michelle Hoffman

Michelle Hoffman, like many children from a broken home, grew up somewhat rebellious and confused, and looked at life with a degree of suspicion and displeasure. Perhaps her mother and father weren't ready for a child and perhaps they were struggling so much themselves that the burdens of life didn't leave any of them with time for everyday happiness.

Michelle Ann Hoffman was born on March 7, 1962 at Riverside Hospital in Toledo to James and Frances Hoffman. The father left and never returned when Michelle was two.

Her mother had no formal education or special skills and was on welfare. Frances struggled to care for both of them, ground down by near poverty, lack of time to spend with her child, and the other burdens of life. Frances decided to relinquish her parental rights, sending Michelle to live with her parents, Bessie and Emanuel Papuchike.

Michelle was 6 when she left to live with her grandparents in East Toledo. She stayed with them until she was 8, when they realized how difficult it was to raise another child. The sister of Michelle's mother, Sonia Ross, and her husband Tom Ross, agreed to take Michelle in as their own. Michelle moved in when she was just beginning to understand life a little.

Michelle was a pretty and intelligent girl.

When she took up residence with her aunt Sonia and Uncle Tom, life would get better. She now had young parents who could better provide the parental care she lacked.

Tom Ross was a Toledo policeman and had been on the department just a short time when he and Sonia took on the responsibility to raise an 8-year-old girl. This was the best thing that could have happened to Michelle. Tom and Sonia had no children of their own but loved Michelle as if she were theirs. It was the first time Michelle had real stability in her young life.

Many psychologists say that children form their characteristic traits as early as age 4, so changing those traits is very difficult – if not impossible. Michelle was sweet and charming at times, but her unstable early childhood would surface occasionally.

When Michelle was 14, her behavior became more incorrigible - talking back, running away from home, and hanging with the wrong people. Even though Tom and Sonia were heartbroken about it, Michelle's mother, Frances, found it necessary to place her in the Lucas County Children's Home, a county-operated residence that served large numbers of orphans, problem, and destitute children. The home was the only alternative because Michelle's biological mother was not capable of caring for her daughter. Michelle developed a history of running away from the Children's Home, as she had while living with her aunt and uncle. On one occasion when Michelle was 16, she was detained and held for shoplifting.

Michelle was not known to use drugs, nor did she ever become involved in any serious criminal activity. She was well-liked by her friends, housemothers at the Children's Home, and all who knew her. She just had a hard time adjusting to what we might call a normal life. Like any young girl, Michelle was looking to be accepted and loved, but even when the Ross family provided that, she still had trouble believing and adjusting.

At times Michelle ran with the wrong kids looking for acceptance, but most of the kids she was drawn to were not able to provide the friendship and direction she needed. Many of them didn't know how to fit in either. The world is full of lonely, confused and unhappy young people, searching for something, anything.

Michelle was a ward of Lucas County while at the Miami Children's Home and remained under its control until June 1981, when she graduated from Penta County Technical High School. She moved back in with Tom and Sonia, staying with them through August. Before long she slipped back into her old ways, and began to show behavioral problems.

Michelle stayed out overnight and away from home for days at a time. She rented a room for a couple of days at a motel and stayed with friends from time to time. She became so incorrigible that her aunt and she quarreled. After so many disagreements, Michelle left to stay with her mother in an apartment on Fourteenth Street near downtown Toledo.

Even though Frances Hoffman kept her place clean, her apartment was in an undesirable area. Prostitutes, drug addicts, derelicts, and other street people lived in the neighborhood. The location made the streets unsafe.

Frances, unemployed and on welfare, was not in a position to support Michelle. She was dating a man who stayed with her on and off. He was a good man who helped Frances financially. Even though Frances knew taking Michelle in would be a strain, she did look forward to seeing her. She had only seen Michelle about three times in the last couple of years. She had visited her only once while Michelle was living in the Children's Home.

Michelle worked for the Toledo Zoo part-time during the summer, after graduating from high school, and had saved some money.

Michelle arrived at her mother's on Aug. 29 with an old worn suitcase that held most of her worldly possessions.

She was there just a short time when she started telling Frances that she wanted to go to a block party with her boyfriend, Wayne Borowski. Wayne was younger than Michelle, only 17, and lived with his parents in south Toledo. He was attending Bowsher High School while working part-time during the summer for the Columbia Gas Company as a maintenance helper.

92

Early that evening, Michelle left in a taxi to attend the block party. This would be the last time Frances would see her daughter alive. They had not spent much time together during Michelle's 19 years, and Frances felt sad for that. After Michelle left for the block party, Frances thought, "I didn't even get a chance to talk to Michelle, nor did Michelle even get a chance to spend the night."

Frances did receive a telephone call from Michelle on Monday, two days later. She said she was with her boyfriend, Wayne. Michelle said she was sorry for not calling, especially after police found the body of Lorena Zimmerman in the weeds off Westwood the day before. The girl had been murdered and Michelle realized that Frances must have been worried for her.

Michelle promised her mother she'd come back to stay, but she never did. Frances said Michelle was wearing blue jeans, brown shoes and a blue plaid blouse when she last saw her. She said Michelle had washed her hair before leaving and noticed she had on a bra and panties when she got dressed.

On Sept. 1 at 10:30 p.m., Wayne took Michelle to work with him at Columbia Gas. Michelle was going to sleep in Wayne's car while he worked, then he would take her to her mother's to get some fresh clothes.

Wayne parked his car in the parking lot and gave Michelle his car keys. Wayne came out for a food break around 3 a.m. and sat in the car with Michelle. They shared his sandwich, then he went back into work. He told Michelle he would see her at 7 a.m. and take her to her mom's. She said she would sleep until then.

When Wayne got off work Wednesday morning, he found his car locked and Michelle gone. She had his keys, so he had to call his older brother, Eddie, to bring his spare keys to him.

Wayne figured that Michelle had decided to walk to her mother's and took the keys, perhaps thinking she would return before he got off work. Wayne went on to school to register and never saw Michelle again. He did not think much of her not being around because she often took off for days at a time. She had many different friends and at times moved from friend to friend, staying with each one for a few days at a time.

When Frances did not hear anymore from Michelle, she called her sister, Sonia Ross. Sonia and Tom became concerned because they had not heard from Michelle either. Tom contacted friends of Michelle but they gave him the impression they didn't want to talk to him. They knew he was a cop and perhaps this was the reason for the silent treatment. When he could not locate Michelle, he made a police report reporting her missing.

Tom was concerned for Michelle because he knew how dangerous it could be for a young woman to be out on her own. He had worked on the Lorena Zimmerman murder earlier and feared something similar could happen to Michelle.

It was a pleasant fall evening on Sept. 17 when 27-year-old Richard Elmer and his wife Kayling went to visit her relatives in north Toledo. They visited for awhile and Richard was ready to go, but his wife wanted to stay a little longer.

Richard decided to go look for rabbits because his wife liked to eat rabbit. His brother-in-law had shown him a wooded area behind Mulberry Park, along the railroad tracks, where he could hunt. He didn't have a gun so he threw rocks at the rabbits – he had managed to kill one this way once before, so he decided to try his luck again.

Richard parked the car sometime around 6:30 p.m. He crawled through a hole in the fence behind the baseball diamond. He walked across the first set of railroad tracks to the wooded area when he saw his first rabbit. Using a rock he pursued his prey.

Richard chased the rabbit through the woods into an area called the Green Belt, also sometimes called the Buckeye Basin. They call it this because there is this stretch of woods and grassy area that winds through the area like a snake slithering through the grass or a river winding its way to a lake.

As Richard ran after the rabbit, he went up a grade, then down into a small gully. Instead of finding the rabbit, he was shocked to see what appeared to be a human body resting beneath a tree. At first he thought it was a dummy or a mannequin, so he poked at it with a stick. When he found that the body was that of a dead human he hurried back to his car.

Richard made his way to a pay phone and called the police. The dispatcher told him to meet a police sergeant at Bancroft and Cherry streets, so he drove there and waited. Sgt. Robert Condon soon arrived and Richard directed him to the scene. At Mulberry Park they were met by a uniform crew. Richard took the officers to where he had discovered the body. The officers saw that the body was lying face down at the foot of a tree in the gully. The body was badly decomposed and the officers sealed off the scene while calling for a detective.

I was working the Detective Bureau when the call came in from the crews at the scene. I drove immediately to the scene.

I didn't know for sure, but I had a gut feeling that the serial killer or killers had struck again. The area where the victim was found was only a few blocks from where Thomas Gordon and Sandra Podgorski were abducted on May 14, 1980. It was only a couple of miles from where victims Stacey Balonek and Daryl Cole were murdered on Aug. 2, 1981, and just a short distance from where Mark Wiler was found on Aug. 17, 1981. All the areas are part of or near the Buckeye Basin and Green Belt area.

When I arrived on the scene I looked at the unknown body. I couldn't tell if the victim was male or female, but by the size it appeared most likely to be a woman. The head was completely decomposed and the rear portion of the skull was missing. What looked like the left hand rested along the left side of the body and a portion of a finger appeared to be missing.

A silver ring band could be seen on one of the fingers. The body was dressed in blue jeans with a thin brown belt, brown moccasin-type shoes, and a greenish blue plaid blouse. The decomposed condition of the body led me to believe the body had been there for two to three weeks.

It was 7:40 p.m. and getting dark. Lucas County Coroner Investigator Joe Inman came to the scene and he agreed with me that the scene should be sealed off, with the victim in place, until daylight, when we could process the scene properly.

The officers were placed in charge and I left for the night with anticipation of returning at first light. In the meantime, I interviewed the man who found the body, Richard Elmer.

After listening to the dispatchers tape and interviewing Richard, there was no doubt in my mind that he was telling the truth about how he found the victim and reported it. Many times the person who reports finding the victim is the one responsible for the killing, but that was not the case with Richard – he was just a good citizen reporting the awful experience he had encountered.

I couldn't sleep that night, hoping the morning would bring evidence to lead to the arrest of the serial killers. The first thing the following morning I organized a search party to comb the area around the body.

I intended to search the surrounding area for evidence while the evidence technicians and coroner's investigator examined the immediate scene. The technicians photographed the entire area while the body was transported to the morgue.

By the condition of the victim's skull, it appeared that she was struck in the back of the head with a heavy object. Several large rocks were collected near the area where the body was located and they were processed for blood, hair and skin tissue. No other serious evidence was located.

Because these homicides were now very high-profile, the media followed detectives around to every crime scene of this nature. I kept them out of the area and they were not allowed in until after the crime scene had been completely processed.

The autopsy was performed on Sept. 21 by assistant coroner, Dr. Steven Fazekas.

The body was that of an unknown white female, 5 feet, 3 inches tall, medium build, with short brown hair. She was not wearing a brassiere or panties. The fact that the victim's belt was unfastened and she was not wearing undergarments led to the suspicion that she may have been – likely was – sexually assaulted.

Two of the front teeth were missing and the left rear portion of her skull had been crushed. The coroner ruled the death a homicide due to blunt force injury to the head.

It was determined that this latest victim was not that of another reported missing woman, who at this time was also a focus of a high-profile investigation. That missing woman was Cynthia Jane

Anderson, white, age 20 and 5 feet, 4 inches tall, 115 pounds, with long brown hair and brown eyes.

Cynthia had been missing from the law offices of Rabbit/Feldstein in north Toledo since Aug. 4, 1981. She was employed as a legal secretary and had opened the office that morning, expecting to work alone until noon when one of the attorneys was to arrive.

A witness saw Cindy entering the office at 8:45 a.m. and another witness knocked on the locked front door of the law office at 10:12 a.m., finding no one there. The office was found locked but there was evidence that Cynthia had completed some paperwork. Her purse, office keys, and car keys were missing. Her car was still parked in front of the building where she was seen parking it earlier by the witness and this is the location where she always parked. No evidence of a struggle was found inside the law office and the building was found secured.

The evidence indicated to me that she had locked up the building and was going to nearby McDonald's, within walking distance, to get something to eat. Her family said she had not eaten breakfast before she left for work.

I theorized she was abducted from the parking lot. She has never been located or seen since. The disappearance of Cynthia didn't match the other homicide/rape cases because she disappeared from the building or parking lot during daylight hours. The serial killers had been only operating at night and even though their victim's bodies were not always easy to find, the killers made no, or very little effort, to hide the bodies. Cynthia had been missing for six weeks.

Even though elements of Cynthia's disappearance were different, one could not completely rule out the possibility that her case could be related to the others. The law office where Cynthia worked was in the vicinity of the Green Belt/Buckeye Basin area and, since Cynthia had been missing for six weeks, it was easy to suspect foul play.

But, really, despite my strong suspicions, it couldn't be said that any of these cases were definitively related – we just couldn't prove that one way or the other. The evidence suggested that most or all were the chilling work by the same murderers, but no one could really be sure until the cases were solved.

Detective Ross went to the morgue to view the latest victim. He feared it was his wife's niece, Michelle Hoffman, so he examined the victim's clothing and jewelry. He thought he recognized the brown leather moccasins – he had moved these shoes so many times while picking up after Michelle, and he was sure the shoes belonged to her.

After learning it might be Michelle, I had photographs taken of all the clothing and jewelry from the body and took these photographs to the home of Michelle's boyfriend, Wayne Borowski. Wayne and his sister, Kim; her husband, David Kubicek, and Wayne's 10-year-old brother, Todd, all identified the clothing, shoes, belt, necklace and silver ring as being Michelle's.

A polygraph examination was given to Wayne. He passed the examination, clearing him of any suspicion in connection with Michelle's death or disappearance.

Sept. 21, through dental records, the dead woman was positively identified as Michelle Hoffman.

It was a sad day for the Toledo Police Division to find that this young murder victim was the niece of one of its own family, Tom Ross. Tom and Sonia took the loss of their niece with much pain. They loved Michelle, and even though she struggled at times through her short life, they believed she was a good person.

Tom and I had worked several years together in homicide, and we both had investigated many murders. Working homicide is extremely difficult because you see the lives of many affected by the loss of their loved ones. It's even tougher when the victims are young. Yet nothing was as wrenching as this one.

Not for the first time since these awful murders had started, I reflected on the belief that everyone has the right and expectation of being safe. It is our job to see that those rights are secure, and at the time, I didn't feel we were doing a very good job.

Sgt. Howard Schlegel, Detective Bill Adams and I, along with other detectives, searched for clues and interviewed all of Michelle's close friends and relatives. We interviewed employers and house mothers at the Children's Home. Sergeant Schlegel and I interviewed Michelle's past boyfriends and people who she stayed with. We checked the motel she stayed at and the friends who visited her there. No new leads.

I knew through 16 years of experience as an investigator that Michelle was not murdered by a prior boyfriend, past friend or relative – she was murdered by someone who was a cold-blooded killer. As sure as I could be about anything, she was yet another victim in the baffling series of homicides that had long since gripped the city with fear – and in a lot of ways mocked those of us whose job it was to stop the killings.

I felt guilty that not only another victim had been sacrificed but, it was now family. I thought, "when will the killings stop?" Why can't we stop them? The long nights to follow would affect my daily activities and my family life. I couldn't sleep. I was tired and grouchy with those around me.

I knew I was not to blame. It didn't matter – I still had this feeling that it was my fault.

Victim – Michelle Hoffman

Chapter 15

Peter Sawicki, Leslie Sawicki, Todd Sabo

Peter Sawicki was a handsome 43-year-old family man, building contractor and real estate developer. Leslie Sawicki, 19, was the apple of her father's eye and he watched over her as though she was still daddy's little girl.

Leslie's boyfriend was Todd Sabo, 21, a strong, energetic member of the University of Toledo wrestling team. Leslie attended Ohio State University and she and Todd spent the summers together as well as some time during the school year.

Todd worked for Peter Sawicki during the summer months cutting grass and doing odd jobs. When home from school, Leslie lived with her parents in the village of Ottawa Hills, a small but affluent suburb of Toledo.

Leslie went out to dinner with her mother and father on Thursday evening, Sept. 17, 1981, and was to see Todd when they returned home. Todd picked Leslie up at her house in his yellow Dodge Van and they went for a ride.

They decided to go to Renee's Nite Club. They arrived around 10:30 p.m., danced and had a beer or two. A little after midnight they left Renee's. Leslie and Todd wanted to spend a little time together before Todd took her home, so they drove to a favorite spot in the parking lot at Terrace View South, an apartment complex owned by Peter Sawicki.

The apartment complex is located in Toledo adjacent to the Ottawa Hills Village line and literally next door to the Ottawa Hills Police Department. They had parked there many times to talk because they felt safe. Since Leslie's father owned the apartment complex, they knew they would not be hassled for parking there. They didn't want to park in front of the Sawicki home because they knew Leslie's mother Marsha would make Leslie come into the house.

Todd parked his van at the east end of 4124 Terrace View South, in a southerly direction. The parking lot is encircled by the separate apartment buildings, each having its own address. The only light was from the spotty parking lot lights, the windows of television watchers, and the evening stars. As Todd and Leslie talked and listened to music their faces were illuminated by the small light coming from the stereo.

It was about half past midnight when the young couple stepped out of the van for a minute. The silence of the night was broken by an intruder armed with a pistol who ordered them back into the van. The gunman was later described as black, 25 to 30 years of age, 5 feet, 10 inches, medium build, short black hair, and a shaggy two inch beard with a small mustache. The gunman was dressed in dark clothing.

Totally surprised, Leslie and Todd did as instructed. Leslie got into the van first, climbing over the driver's seat and taking a seat on the passenger side. Todd entered the van next, climbing over the driver's seat and sitting on the engine cover between the two seats. The gunman's eyes were big and he displayed the confidence of a person who was in complete control. He was cool, and controlling. As he entered the van he directed Todd to get into the back seat.

Although Todd had little fear because of his athletic training, he did as the gunman instructed. While he followed instructions he kept his eyes on the gunman as a wrestler watches his opponent. He was not going to do anything stupid, for fear of Leslie's safety, but he knew in his mind that if the gunman relaxed his guard it would be his turn to take control.

"Give me your money!" The gunman demanded.

Todd replied that they didn't have any money. Leslie said she had $5, but then recalled she had given it to Todd to buy gas for his van. Looking at them in almost a joking manner, the robber said, "I thought you didn't have any money."

"I forgot," Todd said.

With this he handed the robber his wallet containing the $5. The robber laughed, as if to say, "I caught you."

Next he ordered them to get in the rear of the van and sit on the floor, and Leslie and Todd did as instructed. The robber demanded to know what else was in the van and Todd replied he had a tool box and a car stereo.

"What's in here?" The robber asked as he opened the tool box.

"Just my tools," Todd replied.

The robber searched through the tool box, observing various tools and some speaker wire.

"Cut me some speaker wire in three foot lengths," the robber demanded, but Todd replied he didn't have a knife, although there were wire cutters in the tool box. The robber then demanded that Todd use the wire cutters to cut the lengths; Todd was slow in cutting the wire when the robber grabbed the wire cutters from his hand and began cutting the wire himself.

Leslie was ordered to take the wire and to tie Todd's hands behind his back.

Leslie was fumbling with the wire when the robber said, "Here, let me do it."

Todd's hands were tied, and the robber took Todd's belt and tied his feet together.

After Todd was tied, the robber looked at Leslie and said, "There's someone else in here that needs to be tied up."

He ordered her to put her hands behind her back while he tied her hands. Then she put her feet together thinking he would tie her feet like he did Todd's.

The robber looked coldly into her eyes and said, "I am not going to tie your feet."

With that he took a T-shirt he found on the floor of Todd's van and tore it into strips. Part of the shirt was placed in Leslie's mouth, and a second piece was used to tie the gag in place. Leslie was ordered to slide further to the back of the van and to lie on the bed of the van.

The robber then pulled her slacks and panties off, letting them fall to the floor of the van. As the robber began undoing his own trousers, he knelt on the floor of the van near Leslie, who now was horribly aware of just what the assailant intended. She attempted to get up, but the gunman used his free hand to push her to the floor of the van.

Todd pleaded with the gunman not to rape Leslie. He kept repeating, "Please don't do that."

The gunman turned to him and said, "You fucked her, haven't you?"

Todd said yes, "but we are in love."

"It will be the same," the gunman said. "I am just a little darker than you."

As the fear of being raped took over Leslie's thoughts, she fought to free herself, and finally she felt the wire holding her hands tight behind her back come free. She slashed her fingernails toward the gunman's face and eyes, digging and scratching for her life. At almost the same instant, Todd freed his hands and removed the belt from around his ankles. He made a dive for the gunman's gun hand, like a cat attacking its prey. He felt the coldness of the steel pistol and struggled to rip it from the gunman's hand.

As the struggle for the gun grew more intense, Leslie pounded on the assailant. Finally, the gun came free and Todd was – now in control. The feeling of victory came over Todd as he held the assailant by his hair while pulling the hammer back.

Todd placed the gun between the eyes of the robber, telling him, "If you even blink an eye, I am going to pull this trigger."

The roles had suddenly reversed themselves. The once unsympathetic and cold blooded gunman was now crying, whimpering, and begging for his life. He begged that he had a wife and kids to care for. He pleaded with Todd not to shoot him and that if he would let him go he would give him $100 and "run like hell."

Todd held the cocked pistol to the robber's head and said, "Don't move or I will blow your brains out."

"Run for help, Leslie, run for help!" Todd shouted.

Nude from the waist down, she fled the van and ran across the parking lot for one of the adjacent apartment buildings. Leslie's great-grandmother, Victoria Brown, lived in apartment #5 and she would use her telephone to call police. She knew that the Ottawa Hills Police Department was just next door, so surely help was not far away.

Leslie raced to the apartment building, gasping for air as she ran up the stairs to the second floor. When she reached apartment #5 she pounded on her great-grandmother's door, screaming, "Grandma, open the door, please open the door!"

Her grandmother didn't respond, either out of fear or because she was in a deep sleep.

As Leslie searched for help at the other apartments she could hear people scrambling to their doors making sure the locks and deadbolts were secure. It was apparent the people inside were too frightened to open their doors. Finally, the door to apartment #7 was cautiously opened and Kimberly Streets let her in.

Leslie told Kimberly what was happening and asked to use her telephone to call the police.

While Leslie called the Ottawa Hills police, Kimberly got a pair of her jeans for Leslie to put on. Leslie told the dispatcher that a man had just tried to rape her and had a gun. She told him where to send the police, then handed the telephone to Kimberly while running to the window to see what was happening. She saw no one, so she again called the Ottawa Hills police dispatcher. He told her to calm down and that he had already notified the Toledo Police because the offense had occurred in Toledo.

Leslie put on the blue jeans then called her father, Peter Sawicki. She told him what had happened and he said he was on the way.

Five minutes later Leslie peered out the window and saw her father's car parked next to Todd's van. He and Todd had the black man lying on the ground between the van and her father's car. Todd had the man by one arm and her father had him by the other arm.

Leslie left the apartment and ran to the parking lot. Todd was still holding the robber down while her father was kicking and hitting him. Todd didn't have the gun in his hand – Leslie saw it about two feet away from the struggling men.

Leslie's father told her to go and get help.

"Call the police!" Peter Sawicki said.

She turned and ran back toward the apartment building but before she reached the building door, she heard the blast of several gunshots. At the time, Leslie didn't realize the robber had retrieved his gun from where Todd had thrown it and had shot both Todd and her father. She also did not realize that the gunman had also fired shots at her while she fled for help.

As Leslie turned back toward Todd and her father, she saw the gunman running toward her. She opened the apartment building door, ran inside, and slammed the door shut behind her. She looked out the window and saw the gunman getting into a white, medium-size car, which had been parked directly across the parking lot from her, facing out.

Leslie watched as the car turned left, and sped off. She ran out of the building toward Todd and her father just as a Toledo Police car pulled into the parking lot from Terrace View North. Leslie ran to the police car and yelled for the patrolman to chase the white car. She then ran to her father and tried to comfort him until EMS arrived.

"Don't die, Daddy, please don't die," she cried.

It seemed like hours instead of the few minutes it took for medical help to arrive, and Leslie could feel her father slipping away. Finally, help arrived, and both her father and Todd were rushed to Toledo Hospital.

Peter Sawicki was pronounced dead at the hospital.

He had a wound through the neck, with the bullet passing into his left shoulder. There was also a grazing wound to the left upper arm.

Todd had been shot in the neck, head and left shoulder, but he would survive. His pain and suffering would follow him for life. Years later, lead fragments were still lodged in his head and left shoulder.

What had started out as a quiet evening ended up in death and tragedy. The love of a father would lead to the departure of a husband, father, friend, and businessman.

During Todd Sabo's statement to police, he told how, after Leslie ran for help, he continued to restrain the robber. Peter Sawicki arrived and was in a frenzy, attempting to rip the doors off the van to get to Todd.

Sawicki grabbed the robber by the hair and dragged him out of the passenger door.

Sawicki pulled the robber from the van while Todd held the gun at the robber. In his rage, Sawicki struck the robber with his fist and kicked him.

Leslie arrived back on the scene, and she toe kicked the robber. While Todd was struggling with the robber, he looked into the cylinder of the gun, attempting to see if it was loaded. He did not see any bullets and, thinking the gun was empty, he threw it a short distance away onto the grass.

Sawicki told Leslie to go for help and see why the police had not arrived.

As Leslie raced back toward the apartment building, where she had called the police for help earlier, Todd and Peter continued to struggle with the robber.

Todd told investigators that while he and Sawicki continued to fight with the robber, the robber must have worked his way over to where Todd had thrown the gun. The robber grabbed the gun then, Todd heard a bang and felt a sharp pain in his neck.

Three more shots rang out and then Todd heard heavy, raspy breathing coming from Sawicki. Then Todd heard Leslie screaming and the sounds of sirens. Todd looked over at Sawicki and saw a lot of blood covering him. He closed his eyes and the next thing he remembered was hearing the voice of a police officer telling him, "Try not to talk, the life squad is on the way."

Scott Lawhead, 19, was in his apartment on Richards Road at the time of the crime. His building faces the parking lot where it all occurred. It was close to 12:30 a.m. when Scott heard people yelling in the parking lot. He looked out the window, saw a black and yellow van, and heard a lot of yelling.

Then, he saw a young woman run back and forth between the van and the apartment building across the parking lot. He heard four or five shots being fired, then saw a black man run from the van to a white car in the parking lot.

It was a white '78 or '79 Olds Cutlass or Buick, with pin-striping on the side. The man drove onto Terrace View South and turned left heading east toward Richards Road. Scott said the man never turned his car lights on.

It was just before midnight when Daniel Betz pulled into the parking lot where Todd Sabo's van was parked. He parked and walked into his apartment building.

As he walked past the laundry room, he saw a black man with a full beard and mustache standing in the doorway.

Daniel saw that the man did not have any laundry nor did the man say anything. He was sure the man didn't belong there, and told the police about the sighting when he and other residents were interviewed.

Police artist, Robert Poiry and James Carnes, sat down with Todd Sabo and Leslie Sawicki the day after the assaults and drew a suspect composite from their descriptions. This composite closely resembled one of the killers from the composites drawn of the killers who murdered Thomas Gordon and stabbed and raped Sandra Podgorski on May 14, 1980.

I felt the killer in this case was one of the two involved in the other murders. Even with this evidence, some of the other detectives I spoke with believed that whoever killed Peter Sawicki and assaulted Todd Sabo and Leslie Sawicki was not one of the serial killers. They felt there were too many differences between the crimes, but I pointed out that the only difference was that the killer decided to rape Leslie at the scene and in the van, instead of first taking the victims to another location.

All the witnesses and all the neighbors in the various apartment buildings were interviewed in the hope of coming up with a name or a good description of the killer and his car. Area hospitals were asked to report any similar persons who may have been treated for injuries like the ones the killer would have sustained from fighting with Todd and Peter.

After almost three weeks of beating the bushes for witnesses and leads, finally, this case gave us our first big break.

Murder victim – Peter Sawicki

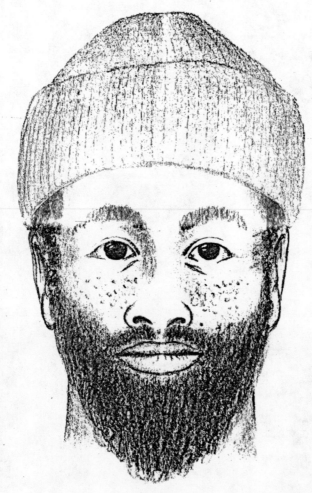

RB#161338
9-19-81 Poiry

Police Drawing of murder suspect – Drawn by Toledo Police
Artist Bob Poiry

Chapter 16
Informant

T oledo Police Juvenile Bureau Detective Dale Siefke received a telephone call on Oct. 6, 1981 from an attorney he had contacts with in the past. The attorney reported that he had received information from a prior client, who wished to remain anonymous. The client said he had information concerning the Sawicki murder and others.

Detective Siefke met with the attorney and the informant at the attorney's home.

The informant related that he personally knew Anthony Cook and suspected Cook as being involved in the Sawicki murder because, he fit the physical description, had visible bruises on his face, and his wife, Peggy Cook, owned a 1978 white Buick Regal like the one the killer fled the scene in. Cook also wore a knit cap and Army jacket that fit the killer's clothing description.

The informant continued that Cook's mother, Marjorie Toles, lived at the Terrace View Apartments where Peter Sawicki was murdered. Cook frequently visited her apartment.

The informant said that Anthony Cook had two sisters, Hazel Marie Madison and Iris Evans, living at the Fountain Circle Apartments in Oregon, Ohio where murder victims Denise Siotkowski and Scott Mouton were discovered shot to death in the trunk of Ms. Siotkowski's car.

Anthony also supposedly admitted to a family member of his involvement in the murder of 12-year-old Dawn Backes. The informant told Detective Siefke that both Anthony and his younger brother Nathaniel were known to have stripped the copper wire from the abandoned State Theater, where Backes was found. He said they then sold the copper to Kripke-Tuschman Industries on Hill Avenue.

After Detective Siefke talked to the informant he contacted Lt. William Kina of the Homicide Unit. Siefke had not been assigned to work any of the homicide cases and had limited knowledge concerning them. Kina and Siefke met with the informant so the lieutenant could establish a relationship with him. However, by this time, the informant was worried for his own safety and was skeptical of continuing his involvement. He said he wanted to work with someone he knew and trusted from the police department – and said he had worked with Sgt. Frank Stiles in the past. He said he trusted Stiles and had a good rapport with him. Kina contacted me, saying the informant had asked to speak with me.

The informant had never been arrested for any violent crimes, but he had been arrested in the past for passing bad checks. He was what we refer too as a "paper hanger." I was the last investigator to arrest the informant for passing bad checks and I was honest with him. I said he might do some time in jail because of the bad check convictions. He did a year in prison, and when he was released he stayed out of trouble and got a job. I would bump into him from time to time and we would talk. I would tell him how important it was to stay out of trouble and encouraged him to walk the straight and narrow. I was something of a mentor to him over the years. The informant got married, maintained his employment, and became a responsible and honest citizen. It made me feel good to see him turn his life around. I felt proud that I may have contributed in some small way.

On October 7, Lt. Kina and I met with the informant behind Wendy's restaurant. He repeated what he had told Siefke.

The informant said he knew Anthony Cook, his sister Pearl, and other family members. After Sawicki's murder he saw the killer's composite in the newspaper and observed the likeness to Cook. The news story indicated that the killer had been injured while struggling with Sawicki and Todd Sabo.

The man said he saw Cook at his home the day after the murder, and Cook had noticeable injuries to his face. He said that after the murder, Cook did not leave his house for at least 10 days, which was unusual because Cook was a roamer and hardly ever stayed around the house. In addition, Cook's wife Peggy owned a 1978 white Buick Regal like the one seen fleeing the scene of the Sawicki murder.

He confirmed his statement to Siefke about the Cooks selling copper wire from the State Theater. I obtained factory copies of checks payable to the Cooks with dates listed from August to November, 1980. I would also suspect Anthony and possibly his brother for the murder of Lorena Zimmerman, who was found in a field near Kripkc-Tuschman on Aug. 30, 1981. She was found nude and had been raped then strangled.

The informant said he also felt Anthony may have murdered the couple found in the trunk of a car at the Fountain Circle Apartments in Oregon, because his sisters Marie Madison and Iris Evans were living in those apartments at the time

During further discussion with the informant, I learned that Anthony Cook had many contacts in or around the areas where other homicides had occurred.

He also lived near the area where murder victim Mark Wiler was bludgeoned to death while tied to a tree.

The informant said Anthony had many problems. He was told by a member of the Cook family that Tony Cook had asked one of his sisters to go to bed and to have sex with him.

Encouraged by the informant, I set out to put the pieces together and to build a case sufficient to arrest Anthony Cook.

I contacted the witness, Scott Lawhead, who saw the killer's white Buick fleeing the scene of the Sawicki murder. Lieutenant Kina and I drove Scott by the Cook's home on October 9. He saw the white '78 Buick and said this could be the car he saw the killer flee in.

I questioned Pearl Erving and her husband, Herman, at their home. Pearl said she thought Anthony could be involved in the murder of Sawicki because he matched the composite and description of the killer she saw on television. She said even though Cook had a lot of problems, she would not want to see her brother go back to prison. She continued that she did not think prison was the answer to anyone's problems.

Pearl called her sisters, Cecelia and Hazel, and asked them to come to her home while I was there. The women agreed and came to the home, where I questioned them.

Both women said that they also feared their brother Anthony could be involved in the murder of Sawicki and others. I showed them the police composites drawn for the Sawicki and the Gordon/Podgorski cases. They all said the composites looked like Anthony.

On Monday, Oct. 12, I again questioned the informant, wanting to find out if Cook had any close friends besides family members. He said the only other person Cook spent time with, besides his brother Nathaniel, was a man he only knew by the nickname of Mayne. He said Mayne lived upstairs in a yellow duplex on Maplewood. I drove the informant to Maplewood where he pointed out the duplex.

Chapter 17

Following the trail

On Oct. 13, Lieutenant Kina and I drove to Mayne's apartment on Maplewood. I saw a street person I knew – also a sometime informant – named Bobby sitting on the porch next door. This home was located right next door to the duplex where Mayne lived.

I called Bobby over, and I asked him who lived upstairs in the duplex. Bobby quickly indicated that he did not want anyone seeing that he was talking to detectives, but he would call me at my office in a few minutes.

He called as promised and the man who lived upstairs was Mayne Kynard. He said he didn't know his real first name but added that he sold drugs.

Bobby said Mayne had the .22 handgun that Peter Sawicki was shot with, and he knew who did the shooting. I told Bobby I wanted to meet with him and arrangements were made to meet behind a church in his neighborhood. Ten minutes later the meeting took place.

Bobby said both he and Mayne hung out at the house next door to Mayne's apartment, occupied by Richard McDuffey.

On Sunday, Oct. 11, at 4 p.m., he said he was talking to Kynard at

McDuffey's house when Kynard invited him to his apartment. He said there was a woman at McDuffey's and she joined them at Kynard's apartment.

Kynard told them he was "holding" the .22-caliber handgun used in the murder of Peter Sawicki. Bobby said Kynard went into another room and reappeared with a brown paper bag. He reached in and pulled out the gun.

Kynard said a friend came by and gave him the gun to hold and said he had shot and killed Sawicki. Bobby claimed Kynard also said the man told him he shot another man with Sawicki.

I knew we were on the right track because what Bobby was reporting matched the evidence and information we already had.

We didn't know it at the time, but we later found out that police technician Gregory Friend had taken a Crime Stoppers call on Oct. 12. The woman on the other end said that a man named Mayne Kynard knew who killed Peter Sawicki and that he had the weapon that was used. She reported that Kynard said the killer's name was Tony, he was a truck driver, and he lived in the Stickney/Central area of north Toledo.

Once we learned of the Crime Stopper call, the information further strengthened what I already knew: Mayne Kynard was the key to an arrest.

Now that I had information from Bobby that the murder weapon was being held at Kynard's apartment on Maplewood, and since this information was supported by the phone tip, a search warrant was prepared and requested.

I took the warrant to Judge Robert Christiansen at Toledo Municipal Court on Oct. 13, at 4:33 p.m. and he signed it.

With a search warrant in hand Lt. Kina and I met with detectives John Tharp and Sam Harris, who, along with a uniform crew, knocked on the door to Kynards home.

No one was home, so we forced the door and searched. We didn't find the .22 we were looking for but we did find a .38-caliber pistol and some ammunition along with a large trunk containing personal items of Anthony and Nathaniel Cook. The trunk contained pictures, including that of a young white woman, costume jewelry, letters from

Anthony to Nathaniel while Anthony was in prison for robbery, and other personal papers of Nathaniel.

The prison letters sent to Nathaniel from Anthony referred to how much he disliked the white prison guards. There was a strong inference of racial hatred within the letters.

At this point, I knew it was imperative to find Kynard before he alerted Anthony about the search. Personal papers found in the apartment made it likely that "Mayne" Kynard was Ernest Kynard. I checked police contacts and found Ernest was wanted on two misdemeanor warrants for bastardy and assault. I picked up the warrants from the Toledo Police Records Section so we could arrest Kynard when we located him.

Although I wasn't familiar with Ernest, I had arrested Kynard's brother, Douglas, along with two other men for the aggravated robbery and murder of Omar Frey at Frey's Pharmacy on Detroit Avenue a few years earlier.

The three went into the pharmacy armed with a sawed-off 12-gauge shotgun and confronted Frey and his wife. Frey's wife was at the register and Omar was in the rear of the pharmacy preparing prescriptions when the robbers entered.

Frey's wife was attacked with a butcher knife and Omar ran to her assistance, only to be shot in the stomach with the shotgun.

Frey died a few days later. I was given the investigation because of my knowledge of possible suspects I had handled in the past. Within a short time, I arrested all three of the killers and obtained full confessions. I also recovered the shotgun used in the homicide. One of the killers was an escapee from an institution at the time of the murder. All of those men were incarcerated at the time Peter Sawicki was murdered, so I knew none of them could be involved in any of these homicides.

The one who could tell us what we needed to know was Ernest Kynard.

Armed with the two misdemeanor warrants outstanding for Kynard, Lt. Kina and I began searching for him. We went to the house located next door to Kynard's, the home of Richard McDuffey.

When we arrived we found McDuffey at home, along with the

informant, Bobby. I took McDuffey into the kitchen to talk because he appeared apprehensive in front of Bobby. After calming him he told me what he knew.

McDuffey said Kynard lived next door and came over all the time to talk and have a few drinks. He said Kynard liked to talk and he told him, Bobby, McDuffey's son Lee, his house companion John Pryor, and a lady friend of theirs, Beverly Day, about having the gun that Peter Sawicki was murdered with.

Kynard was at his house on Sunday Oct. 11, about 4 p.m., and told them he had the Sawicki murder weapon. Kynard had said he was given the murder weapon by his friend, Tony. McDuffey went on, saying, Tony's wife was a school teacher and had a white car and that the car was used in the murder. He said he heard Tony's mother was a very religious person.

McDuffey said Kynard had claimed that he had the murder weapon in his apartment. I asked McDuffey if his friend, Bev Day, nicknamed Penny, was the woman who had called Crime Stoppers with information about Kynard having the murder weapon. He said yes, she told him she had called. McDuffey was advised that he should watch for Kynard and to call me as soon as he saw him. He said he would. I also told McDuffey to have Bev Day call me as soon as he saw or heard from her.

I later talked to McDuffey's house companion, John Pryor, at the police department.

Pryor said he lived with McDuffy and he knew Kynard and his friend, Tony Cook. He said both men visited their home, Kynard more frequently.

Pryor said Kynard came over almost every night and would tell everyone everything he knew. Pryor said he liked to talk.

He went on to say that on the morning after Peter Sawicki was murdered, he heard voices coming from behind Kynard's apartment next door. It was a warm morning and he had his bedroom window open. It was just getting daylight when he heard people talking and looked out the window to see who it was.

"Kynard and Cook were standing there talking," Pryor said. They were standing by a light-color Buick he later found out belonged to

Cook's wife. He said he had been to Cook's home with Kynard and knew both Cook and his wife, Peggy. He said he went to the same church on Bronson Street that Peggy Cook attended – Tony Cook was rarely at church but, his wife was there often.

Pryor said while he was watching Cook and Kynard, he saw Cook reach into his front pocket and pull out a gun, handing it to Kynard. Pryor claimed he heard Kynard say, "Man, you shouldn't have done that," and that Kynard said "you're in a lot of trouble." Pryor said he couldn't make out anything else in their conversation and soon after, they went into Kynard's apartment.

Pryor claimed that at about 9:30 that same morning, Kynard came over and spouted the whole story to himself, McDuffy and Beverly Day. He said Kynard told them that Cook gave him the gun that he had shot a man in Ottawa Hills with.

Kynard had said Cook wanted him to hold the gun for him so he wouldn't get caught with it.

Pryor said Kynard's story was that the gun was a .22 and Cook told him that he had gone to the Ottawa Hills area to commit a robbery, but ended up trying to rape a girl. Cook allegedly told Kynard that two white men overpowered him and one of the men got the gun away from him. He said the man looked into the barrel of the gun and when he didn't see any bullets in the cylinder of the gun he apparently thought the gun was empty so he threw the gun into the grass.

According to Pryor, Kynard went on: Cook said that while the men were kicking and beating him he was able to work his way over to where the gun had been thrown, and he scooped it up. Cook said he shot the two men then shot at the girl, who was running toward some apartments. Cook said he only got $5 for his troubles, according to the story. Pryor told me he later heard about the Sawicki murder on the news and realized Kynard wasn't just making it all up.

Kynard had also claimed that Cook had confided in him that he had murdered three other people and had raped four other girls, including a girlfriend of Kynard's. Kynard had said that Cook's brother, from Columbus, was involved in some robberies as well. Pryor told me Kynard did not mention the name of Cook's brother, but said he went back to Columbus because he was worried the police were also after him. Kynard said Cook's brother kept a big trunk at his apartment and there was some jewelry and watches in the trunk. He said Cook and his brother told him that they had committed some street robberies and that was where the jewelry came from.

I asked Pryor if Kynard told him where the gun used to murder Peter Sawicki was hidden. No, Pryor said, but Kynard told him he had a .38-caliber hidden in his apartment. This was the gun we found in Kynard's apartment with the search warrant.

I asked Pryor what else he knew about Cook. He answered that once when he was talking with Cook, the man had told him his wife was a school teacher and that he worked driving semi trucks.

On that same day I interviewed Pryor, Oct. 14, I got a call from Beverly Day. She admitted she was the one who called Crime Stoppers with the information that Kynard had the gun Sawicki was murdered with. She agreed to meet me.

Lt. Kina and I met Day and she said she had just seen Kynard on Delaware near Lawrence. She said he was wearing a white knit cap, brown suede jacket, light colored pants and tan shoes. She said he had a large afro that stuck out from under his white cap. I said, "We will talk to you later," then sped off in search of Kynard.

Sgt. Frank Stiles makes a friend while checking a
motorcycle for stolen. The motorcycle was discovered
during his search for witnesses and suspects.

Chapter 18

Ernest (Mayne) Kynard

In the central city, we spotted Ernest Kynard getting into the car of a man I knew, Christopher Yowpp. Lt. Kina was driving and I yelled, "Pull in front of the car." As the lieutenant blocked the car, I jumped out and confronted Kynard, arresting him on the warrants for bastardy and assault. We took him to the Toledo Police Division where I interrogated him. I read Kynard his rights and he signed a waiver agreeing to make a statement.

Ernest Kynard appeared a little apprehensive about telling me what he knew, and at first he denied any knowledge of the murder weapon involved in the murder of Peter Sawicki. He said he had never said anything to anybody about the gun, and claimed he didn't hear any statements from Anthony Cook about the murder of Peter Sawicki, the shooting of Todd Sabo, or the attempt to rape Leslie Sawicki.

I confronted Kynard with the fact that he had talked to several people who went on record as saying he had shot his mouth off, and that he had even claimed to be holding the gun for Cook. I pointed out he could be arrested for tampering with evidence and obstructing justice if he failed to cooperate. It was then that he said he would tell the truth.

Kynard explained he was friends with Cook, having known him and his family since the early '60s. They lived near each other but did not become really good friends until Cook was released from the penitentiary in November 1979. When Cook got out of prison, the two became closer and Cook sometimes stayed with him. Kynard also said he was good friends with Cook's brother, Nathaniel, who lived in Columbus and was an over-the-road trucker.

Kynard said Nathaniel would stop by his apartment when in town and sometimes stayed with him. "The trunk police found in my apartment belonged to Nathaniel," Kynard said, but both Anthony and Nathaniel kept things in it.

I asked Kynard to give a detailed statement concerning the possession of the gun used in the Sawicki murder and also what Anthony Cook told him about the murder.

Kynard said he knew that Cook's wife Peggy owned the white Buick Regal used by Cook during the murder. Kynard's girlfriend, Rhonda Butts, spent the night with him and when they got up on Sept. 18, his girlfriend got ready for school and left. He heard a noise, then heard someone shouting for him from the backyard. He looked out of the back window and saw Cook standing below the window. The white Regal was parked in the back and Cook was trying to get his attention.

Kynard opened the window and asked what he wanted. "We need to talk," Cook replied. Kynard let him in through the back door. Cook looked tired and had bruises on his badly swollen face. Kynard asked what happened. "I got into trouble and was beaten up," Cook said.

Cook told about how, shortly after midnight, he was riding around Ottawa Hills looking for someone to rob, when he spotted a van in a parking lot. A young white man and woman were standing by the van and as he pulled into the lot the couple entered the van. He parked his wife's car nearby and quietly approached the van. Cook's account to Kynard about what happened after that pretty much squared with the scenario laid out by Leslie and Todd.

Cook told him he didn't know what to do or where to go after he escaped the scene because, he knew he had to come up with an explanation for his injuries. He needed time to think, to prepare a story, so he drove to Kynard's apartment and waited until morning.

Kynard told Cook he should shave his beard to make it harder to identify him.

Cook responded that he had his beard all his life and, if he suddenly shaved it off, his wife and others would know something was wrong. Cook showed Kynard his .22 revolver with white handles, saying, "This is the gun I shot them with." Cook asked for a paper bag to conceal the gun. Kynard said he and Cook took the bag to the backyard, and they hid it behind a tree near Kynard's garage.

Cook also handed over a box of bullets and asked Kynard to hide them for him. He put the bullets behind the front stairs carpet on the fourth stair.

Later Kynard called Cook and told him that the police had searched his house with a warrant; Cook said he didn't have to worry because the police didn't have anything on him. Cook asked if the police had found his gun and he told him that he didn't think so. "Cook was too afraid to touch the gun for fear the police were watching the house," Kynard explained.

Cook said he was going to leave the gun where it was, but if the police got too close, he would come get the gun and leave town. Cook said if he had to, he would shoot it out with the police.

I asked Kynard if he would sign a search warrant waiver, and take us back to his apartment to find the murder weapon and box of shells. He agreed. We found the Rohm .22-caliber six-shot revolver with white handle grips hidden behind the tree. The gun was empty and one of the grips was missing its insignia. We found the box of .22 bullets hidden behind the stair carpet.

At the police station, I took a taped statement from Kynard, I then booked him for the two misdemeanor warrants. He was released on his own recognizance pending a court hearing. He was told not to talk to anyone about the investigation until I had a chance to get warrants for Cook. The gun and bullets were turned over to technician Larry Mallory so he could check the items for fingerprints. It turned out that no prints of value were removed from the gun or bullets. The street smart killer had wiped the gun and bullets clean.

I checked to see if the gun was stolen, but no stolen report was found. Ballistics was performed to see if the bullets in the Sawicki/Sabo case, Cheryl Bartlett shooting, and Denise Siotkowski and Scott Moulton murders matched.

Because of the poor condition of the recovered bullet fragments, ballistics could only show that this could have been the same weapon involved in all the shootings. Experts could testify that the gun used in all these shootings was a Rohm .22 revolver, like the one recovered from Kynard, but they couldn't positively say it was the same gun.

Kynard was given a polygraph test concerning a connection to any murders or crimes with Anthony or Nathaniel Cook, and the results showed he was not involved.

After I saw to it that Kynard was taken home, I sat down for a moment to collect my thoughts and composure. I knew, finally, the day had come that we were about to arrest the perpetrator of Peter Sawicki's murder – and maybe many others I believed were committed by the same killers. I thought, dear God, can this be the end to the killing and suffering?

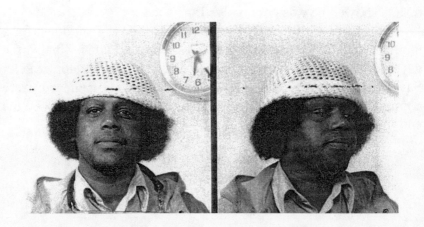

Witness Ernest (Mayne) Kynard

Chapter 19

The Arrest

N ow armed with sufficient information and evidence to obtain arrest and search warrants for Anthony Cook, I started the paperwork.

I prepared search warrants for the white Buick used in the murder of Peter Sawicki and assaults on Leslie Sawicki and Todd Sabo; Cook's white and green pickup truck, and the Cooks' home on Homer Street. At 9:30 p.m., I took the warrant applications to the home of Judge Christiansen, who signed the affidavits.

I also prepared and obtained arrest warrants for Anthony charging him with the aggravated murder of Peter Sawicki, attempted murder and aggravated robbery of Todd Sabo, and attempted rape of Leslie Sawicki.

After talking to Kynard, friends and family members of Cook, I knew he drove trucks for O'Dell Edwards, the boyfriend of Cook's sister, Maryann. Edwards had a vacant house located on N. Crissey Road in suburban Lucas County. Cook would sometimes do work on the trucks at this house, which they called the Ponderosa.

While I was obtaining the warrants, I had Lt. Kina, Det. Tharp and Det. Harris set up surveillance on the Ponderosa. They found that Cook was at that location.

I had the warrants. Accompanied by fellow detectives John Connors and McDavid McCorvey, I headed for the Ponderosa on North Crissey Road. Before we got there we received a radio transmission that Cook had left the premises and was on the road. I wanted Cook to travel back to Toledo before we arrested him and executed the search warrant for his truck – the warrants were issued in the jurisdiction of the City of Toledo and I didn't want any legal foul-ups.

Lt. Kina and Det. Tharp kept me informed of Cook's location and when he reached Toledo, we stopped him. Police cars boxed in the truck while we got out with guns drawn. We had reason to believe we were dealing with a hardened serial killer; there was no reason not to treat him as anything but armed and dangerous.

Cook was ordered from his vehicle and he gave up without a fight. No gun was found on his body or in the truck. I arrested him, stating the charges listed in the warrants, and we took him to the police station. His truck was towed to the police station garage so it could be searched.

Cook's employer, O'Dell Edwards, had been following in his car and stopped behind Cook's truck when we arrested him. I asked Edwards to come to the Toledo Police Division to talk with me and he agreed.

While Cook's truck was being processed for victims' fingerprints, it was also photographed and searched for evidence from the various reported murders and crimes. I first interviewed O'Dell Edwards, and then Cook himself.

When the police technician photographed and printed Cook's truck, I had detectives execute the search warrant for the pickup. The only evidence of value found was a tan knit cap and a greenish knit ski-mask that matched the general description of caps worn by the perpetrator in some of the other crimes. Also, some keys were confiscated from Cook. I wanted to match them with keys taken from the various victims.

During my interview with Edwards, he told me he had known Cook since 1975 and that Cook's sister, Maryann, was his girlfriend. Cook had been working for him for a year or two, driving tractor-trailer rigs. He said he had three trucks and was self-employed, with some of his business coming out of Detroit. Edwards said Cook had driven out-of-state for him in Indiana, Ohio, Michigan, Tennessee, and Kentucky. He said sometimes Cook was accompanied by another driver he employed by the name of Ison Gordon.

I later questioned Gordon and he confirmed that he had worked with Cook, making over-the-road deliveries. When asked if Cook had ever assaulted any young girls while he was with him, Ison said no, but that he hadn't taken that many trips with him. "Did Cook ever tell you about killing or raping anyone," I asked. No, he replied. Did Cook ever pick up hitchhikers while they were on the road? "No," said Gordon.

I asked Edwards if he was aware of Cook being involved in the murder of Peter Sawicki or any other crimes, and he said no. My informant had told me that Edwards was aware that Cook murdered Sawicki, but Edwards wouldn't admit it.

By the time I finished interviewing Edwards, it was 11:35 p.m. It was time to question Anthony Cook.

Prior to interrogating any suspect, especially one suspected of being a serial killer, the investigator tries to know as much about him as he can. I studied his past police contacts, did a complete history check of his family, friends, education, habits, likes and dislikes. I knew I was most likely dealing with a sociopath. They have little or no feeling for others and think nothing of lying, stealing, and manipulating their victims. They can be charming or use intimidation and violence to gain control. They have no empathy for others or remorse about what they do.

I interrogated Cook at the Detective Bureau after advising him of his rights and after he signed a waiver-of-rights form. Cook was asked if he was under the influence of any alcohol or drugs and he said no.

"How far did you go in school?" I asked.

"I attended Scott High School through the ninth grade, then finished my GED while in prison," he said. "I also attended one year of college at Columbus Technical Institute in Columbus, Ohio."

I told Cook he was being arrested for the aggravated murder of

Peter Sawicki, attempted murder and aggravated robbery of Todd Sabo, and attempted rape of Leslie Sawicki. He was given copies of the warrants and he said he understood what he was being charged with. There was no expression of fear on his face – he appeared collected, as if being arrested was expected.

I had Cook take off his shirt and roll up his pant-legs. I was looking for bruises, cuts or scratches that he might have received while fighting with Todd and Peter. There were marks on his knees and shins. It had been a month since the Sawicki murder, so most of the wounds had time to heal.

Even though these wounds had started to heal, they did not appear to be over a month old. I asked Cook where and how he received the injuries. He said it was while getting in and out of his truck. 'The truck cab is high up and sometimes I hit my knees and shins while getting in and out," he said.

Also found during the examination was a large bump behind his left ear. It appeared to be a birth deformity. When Janie Fall was assaulted by a black man while walking home from work on June 22, 1981, she noticed a similar bump behind the left ear of her attacker.

Cook was wearing a khaki green shirt and it met the general description of what a suspect was wearing during some of the offenses. I confiscated the shirt and later placed it in the police property room along with other evidence that had been collected.

I asked Cook where he was on the morning of Sept. 18 around 12:30 a.m., and he said he couldn't remember. He had no alibi and only said he was usually working or at home.

I told him that victims and witnesses described the Sawicki killer and a drawing was made. The artist composite matched him closely, I said. Cook admitted that he was aware of the Sawicki murder, and agreed that he looked like the composite.

I advised Cook that his close friend, Ernest "Mayne" Kynard, had implicated him in the murder of Sawicki and the assaults on Todd and Leslie. I told Cook I had the murder weapon he left at Kynard's home after the shootings. I said that Kynard told me about the events of that night, but that I wanted to hear Cook's side of the story.

"Tony, only you can tell what really happened," I said.

Cook looked at me. "I would like to tell you and give you my side of what happened, but I don't know what to do."

He asked if he could ask a question off the record. I said I don't deal off the record and that anything he asked or said could be used against him. Cook said he didn't want to ask a particular question if it could be used against him in court. I finally agreed to answer the question – off the record – and advised him that I was doing this in the hope that afterwards he might consider giving a full statement.

"Do you think a three-time loser would ever see daylight again, on this type of crime, when he goes to jail?" he asked.

My answer was that it depended on the offense and the circumstances; I had seen two-and three-time losers go to jail for many years and I had seen first-offenders go to jail for just as long. On the other hand, I had seen repeat offenders get out without too long of an incarceration.

"Look, Tony, you are being charged with very serious crimes and you can be incarcerated for a long, long time," I said. "Sentencing is strictly up to the court and I can't promise you anything." I told him I knew he was involved in several other murders and crimes, and I went over the list with him. I said, "I can assure you of this Tony; if you tell me everything, there will be a lot of parents, relatives, and friends of the victims who will receive closure. You can do something positive and give back a little of which you have taken - peace of mind. Think of yourself as a parent, relative or loved one of your victims. Wouldn't you want to finally know the truth and have closure?"

I again asked Cook if he would be willing to make a full disclosure of the facts in the case. He said he would like to talk but wanted to think about it for a while. "Maybe later I will give a statement," Cook said.

I left him sitting in the interrogation room. I thought if we left him alone for a short time maybe he would be willing to confess to all the crimes he had committed. Before I could get in there with him again, Cook's attorney, Alan Kirshner, came to the bureau and said he wanted to see his client. Members of Cook's family found out he'd been arrested so they hired Kirshner to represent him. I wasn't happy that I wouldn't get another chance to interrogate Cook, knowing he was close to confessing.

Once the attorney appeared on Cook's behalf and Cook requested to speak with Kirshner, I was prevented from conducting any further questioning.

After Kirshner stopped the questioning, my squad and I went to the home of Anthony and Peggy Cook on Homer Street to execute the remaining search warrants. On this dark cool morning, only dim lights could be seen coming from the small, one-story house.

It was 1:40 a.m. on Oct. 15 when we searched the home in the presence of Peggy Cook. She gave the impression of a woman who knew why we were there. Next was the search of Peggy's white Buick. Assorted clothing was confiscated from the house, and a black club was confiscated from under the front seat of the car. The clothing matched the general description of clothing worn by the killers during some of the murders we thought might be traced to Cook. Peggy Cook said the club belonged to her and she used it for protection.

She said she knew nothing of Tony's alleged crimes. He was gone a lot driving a truck for Edwards, and many nights he stayed out late working on the trucks at Edwards' vacant house. Peggy Cook spoke in an educated manner and she had a polite, quiet way about her. She showed no disrespect for the police.

The evidence was collected, marked, and placed in the police night property room.

We finally went home for a short night's rest, but I couldn't sleep. I knew we had to move fast with a lineup later that day, before the news media plastered Cook's face all over the newspaper and TV. If Cook's picture was shown before the lineup, it could taint a good identification. I knew Leslie Sawicki and Todd Sabo would positively identify Cook because of the amount of time they spent with him on that awful morning of Sept. 18. I had other victims who had gotten a good look at their attackers, and I believed there was a very good chance of other identifications as well.

Chapter 20

The Line-Up

I t was 6 a.m. Thursday, Oct. 15, and I had only been home for an hour and a half since arresting Anthony Cook and searching his home and vehicles. I had tried to sleep, but was too exhausted, thinking about the upcoming line-up.

"Up and at 'em, Stiles, no time to waste," I thought. "Shower, shave, and a clean suit is all you need."

Out the door, drive to work, and then start organizing the witnesses and victims needed for this all-important line-up.

It was our day, I thought. Those who had lived to tell their story would now get the chance to point out at least one of the killers. All the evidence pointed to the fact that Anthony was the primary killer in the murders, but there were two savages involved during some of the assaults.

I was sure Nathaniel Cook was involved in some of the murders, but he wasn't the leader in the brutal killings and rapes. He was a follower. Since Anthony made no full disclosure about the killings, the evidence against Nathaniel was weak. I decided to make our case against Anthony, and then go after Nathaniel.

The victims who had survived their attackers, and those who were witnesses in the crimes, were notified to appear at the line-up. Leslie

Sawicki and Todd Sabo, Janie Fall, Charles Hackenberg and Laurie Specht, Sandra Podgorski and Arnold Coates, were all contacted. Arnold Coates' girlfriend, Cheryl Bartlett, was in the hospital receiving more treatment for the wound she suffered during the rape and shooting.

Line-ups have to be fair; there must be at least six individuals in the line-up, including the suspect, and they must be of the same race. They must be similar in physical stature and complexion. Hairstyles, mustaches, and beards are also taken into account when preparing line-ups. This time around, I was pleased, thinking that if someone didn't know their suspect, they would surely not be able to make an identification. The line-up was held at the Lucas County Jail at 3:03 p.m.

The defendant's attorney, Alan Kirshner, was present. Lucas County Prosecutors Curtis Posner and George Runner were there, too. Sheriff's Deputy Trilby Cashin set up the line-up, controlling the movement of the men.

All the victims and witnesses were kept separate from each other so they would not influence each other's identification. Leslie Sawicki went first. The suspects were aligned in a room with a one-way glass window – separating the witness from the suspects. Just like on TV, the witnesses could see the suspects but the suspects couldn't see the witnesses.

I told Leslie to take her time while studying the men. She started shaking and a look of fear came over her face as she said without hesitation, "He's the Number 2 suspect."

Anthony Cook.

"One down," I thought. "Tony, your reign of terror is over. We got you, it's time to pay the price."

Todd Sabo was next. Surely he would be able to identify Cook, I anticipated. Todd spent the most time with him. I wasn't disappointed, Todd took one look and immediately said, Number 2. With a strong tone of conviction, Todd said, "I will never forget his face."

Two down, and things couldn't be going any better.

The young couple who had been confronted by an armed robber

in Charles Hackenberg's car were next. First Charles, followed by his girlfriend, Laurie Specht. Again, like picking out a family member, they positively identified Cook.

Janie Fall took her turn. She was the young woman walking home from work in the late evening when an attacker grabbed and dragged her toward a wooded area. She got a good look at the attacker because she fought with him face to face. She was one of the fortunate victims because she escaped with only bad memories and mental scars. With tearful emotion, she pointed to Cook, saying, "He's Number 2." I asked if there was any doubt and she said, "No, Mr. Stiles, I'm sure."

By this time the prosecutors had a slight twinkle in their eyes and a smile on their faces. The defense attorney was pacing back and forth in the viewing room not hiding his disappointment. I knew he was thinking this was not good, not good at all.

There was a good reason why the victims were so successful in identifying Cook. He had spent a considerable amount of time with each victim, probably thinking that he didn't care if they saw his face because they wouldn't live to tell. But with these victims, things didn't go as Cook had planned; they escaped and they did tell.

Next Arnold Coates was brought into the viewing room. He was the boyfriend of Cheryl Bartlett. Arnold only saw one of his attackers because after being confronted by the first robber, a stocking cap was put on his head and pulled down over his eyes

It was clear Arnold was having difficulty making identification. He picked out the Number 6 suspect who was not Anthony Cook, but looked like him. I interviewed this person later, just to make sure he was not involved. He had an alibi for the time the offense occurred and was also given a polygraph examination, which he passed.

Even though Cheryl Bartlett could not attend the line-up, she was given the opportunity to view the suspects. I sent Detective Jim Carnes out to see her later, and he showed her two sets of photo-arrays consisting of eight photographs in each. The arrays included the pictures of Anthony and Nathaniel Cook. She made a positive identification of Anthony, but was unable to identify Nathaniel.

After Arnold Coates viewed the line-up, one of the few living victims, who probably had suffered the most, stepped into the viewing room. Sandra Podgorski had been through so much during and since that early morning of May 14, 1980, when her boyfriend was shot to death and she was raped, stabbed repeatedly with an ice-pick type of weapon, then left for dead in her boyfriend Thomas Gordon's car.

Sandra viewed the six subjects and asked that the men turn to their sides for a profile. She asked that they say something and all the men were asked a question so she could hear their voices. She said she could not be sure but indicated No. 2 looked like one of the killers who had assaulted her. She was asked to look at the men very closely and was again asked if she saw anyone who had assaulted her. She said she couldn't be sure.

I thought Sandra recognized Cook as one of her assailants, but just couldn't commit herself. Since she had made a wrong identification earlier in the investigation with Sheriff's Investigator Gary Heil, she may have been hesitant to identify Cook.

When the line-up was over, even though it had been very successful against Cook, we had a lot of work to do. Nathaniel Cook was still out there, and many of the crimes still had to be solved.

I believed Sandra Podgorski knew her attackers and although she did not positively identify Anthony Cook at the line-up, I decided to take photo-arrays of Nathaniel and Anthony Cook to her and see if she might be able to identify them in a more comfortable atmosphere.

Sandra hadn't seen a line-up which included Nathaniel Cook because, he had not been arrested. I made arrangements for us to meet at her new place of employment, Ma Cheri Beauty Salon. I showed her two separate photo-arrays with eight photos each, including Anthony and Nathaniel Cook.

When Sandra gave her original description of the killers, soon after they murdered her boyfriend, and raped and stabbed her, she described the killers almost as if she had taken a picture of them. She even described the army jacket Nathaniel was wearing – the same kind of jacket he was wearing in the police photograph she was now viewing.

Sandra looked at the array containing the photo of Nathaniel Cook. Her eyes appeared to focus on Nathaniel's photo but she did not make the ID. She was then shown the array with Anthony Cook, and she picked him out as being the same person she had seen in the line-up. Sandra said he looked like the man who was called "Tony" by the other killer during the assaults. "He looks like the one who stabbed me," she said.

I showed her a photograph of the line-up and again she picked out the No. 2 suspect, Anthony Cook, as looking like the man who stabbed her. "He is the same man I picked out in the line-up," she said.

"I know. But can you say he is one of the men who raped you and the one who stabbed you?" I asked.

"He looks like the man."

Again, I thought Sandra recognized Anthony Cook as the man who stabbed her. She had also focused on Nathaniel's photograph and I felt she may have recognized him as the second killer, but again, she did not make positive identifications.

I also showed Sandra two rings of keys containing both house and car keys. One of the rings was confiscated from Ernest Kynard's home at the time we executed the search warrant for his apartment, and one was confiscated from Anthony Cook at the time of his arrest.

Sandra looked at the keys and said none of them belonged to her, but she could not remember what Thomas Gordon's house and car keys looked like. Gordon's house and car keys were stolen by the killers. Sandra said that Tom's brother, Walter Gordon, now owned Tom's car and would know if the keys fit the car. Walter Gordon was a Lucas County sheriff's deputy assigned as a bailiff with the Toledo Municipal Court. After I left Sandra, I drove to the court and spoke with Walter. We took the keys and tried them in the locks of Tom's car, the one in which he and Sandra were abducted in. They didn't fit.

As I was driving back to the Police Division I thought it would have been nice if the keys had fit and if Sandra had made positive ID's of the Cook brothers. If she had been able to do this, we could have arrested both brothers and cleared another one of these awful cases. But the identifications weren't conclusive and the keys didn't fit Thomas Gordon's car.

No arrest could be made at this time.

Chapter 21
Grand Jury Hearing

T he grand jury hearing was convened on Oct. 19. Seven witnesses entered the grand jury room one by one, where they each testified. After a short time the jurors returned a seven-count indictment against Anthony Cook. He was indicted for the aggravated murder of Peter Sawicki, attempted murder of Todd Sabo, aggravated robbery of Todd Sabo, and attempted murder and attempted rape of Leslie Sawicki.

In addition to the five-count indictment involving the Sawicki and Sabo cases, two other indictments were handed down. Anthony Cook was indicted for aggravated robbery in connection with his attempt to rob Charles Hackenberg while in his car with his girlfriend, Laurie Specht, on July 23, 1981.

The final and seventh indictment was for the abduction of Janie Fall, who Anthony Cook dragged off the street into a wooded area as she walked home from work on June 22, 1981.

The abductions and robberies of Cheryl Bartlett and her boyfriend, Arnold Coates, and the attempted murder and rape of Ms. Bartlett on Jan. 27, 1981, was not presented to the grand jury because Cheryl had not yet made her identification of Anthony Cook. She had not yet been contacted and had not been shown the photo-array until after the grand jury hearing.

Once Cheryl made her identification, the prosecutors decided to hold the cases until after the trial of Anthony Cook for the Sawicki/Sabo cases. If Cook was convicted in the Sawicki/Sabo cases, he most likely would receive life in prison, and a trial for the Bartlett/Coates charges wouldn't be necessary.

The prosecutors' didn't want to put Bartlett and Coates through the stress of the court hearings unless it was absolutely necessary.

The arrest and indictments of Anthony Cook were gratifying, but the investigation wouldn't be completed until Nathaniel Cook was arrested and the other murders and rapes solved.

Chapter 22
Nathaniel Cook

Anthony Cook was an introvert and the only people close to him were his family and his friend, Mayne Kynard. Cook's best and closest friend was his brother, Nathaniel. With that in mind, I felt that the other killer who was with Anthony on some of the murders had to be either Nathaniel or Kynard.

As for Kynard, I eliminated him as a suspect by giving him a polygraph examination and by thoroughly checking his movements and alibis during the times the murders and rapes were committed.

Nathaniel Cook is nine years younger than Anthony, and friends and relatives said he looked up to his older brother. It was said that Nathaniel would do anything for Anthony. Murder and rape is a stretch for "anything," but the evidence pointed in that direction.

At the time most of the murders/rapes were committed, Anthony Cook was 31 and 32 years old, while Nathaniel was 21 and 22. Some family members and friends indicated that Anthony had a strong hatred for white people. I had found several letters from Anthony to his brother, which he wrote from prison during his past incarcerations. In the letters Anthony told "Moby," Nathaniel's nickname, that he hated the white prison guards. I found the letters in a large green Army-type trunk Nathaniel kept at Kynard's apartment.

Nathaniel later told me this was his trunk.

Some said Anthony was oversexed and had even made overtures toward his sisters.

If one was baking a cake of crime – with murder, sexual assault and hatred mixed in – the brothers were all the ingredients one would need.

Digging into Nathaniel's background, I found that when not in the company of Anthony, he was a constructive citizen. He worked and was well liked.

Nathaniel attended high school but dropped out. When the murders and rapes occurred he was living in Columbus, traveling back and forth to Toledo during 1980 and 1981. When he came to Toledo he stayed with Kynard, Anthony, or various family members.

The Cooks' mother was a very religious person and made the children attend church. She did the best she could, but raising such a large family was a struggle and created many problems.

Nathaniel had no criminal convictions, but he had been arrested on March 21, 1980, for a misdemeanor drug offense. It was known that Nathaniel used drugs sometimes and he liked to drink.

Nathaniel obtained his last driver's license in Toledo while living with Anthony and that license had an expiration date of Oct. 25, 1983. At that time he was driving a gray Ford Thunderbird, which belonged to his girlfriend, Darnita Zeigler.

Nathaniel's last employment was with Madison Brothers Trucking Company in Toledo. He was a semi-truck driver who drove to various states hauling steel and other loads. He got this job through Floyd Madison, who used to be married to the Cooks' sister, Hazel Marie Madison.

A few years before, Nathaniel traveled back and forth to California. He had a girlfriend in Diamond Bar, Calif. by the name of Benita.

On the morning of Oct. 28, Nathaniel and Anthony's wife Peggy, came to the Police Division in an attempt to gain a release for Anthony's pickup truck he had been arrested in. I was out on the street interviewing witnesses when Lt. Kina called me to make sure it was OK to release it. I told him that the truck could be released but that I wanted to make an appointment to interview Nathaniel and Peggy Cook. A meeting was arranged for Oct. 29 at 11 a.m.

The time had come for me to interview Nathaniel Cook. I figured he would show up for this interview because he wouldn't want to draw suspicion to himself. If he refused he would look guilty and that was the last thing he would want to do.

As anticipated, Nathaniel showed up on schedule, and Peggy Cook was with him. I questioned Peggy first, alone in the interviewing room. She was friendly but nervous. Peggy said she had no idea that Anthony was involved in the murder of Peter Sawicki and the assaults on Leslie Sawicki and Todd Sabo. She denied knowledge of any other murders or assaults Anthony may have committed. She said her husband did stay out late and was gone for days at a time driving truck, but she thought he was just making deliveries.

"Peggy," I said, "there must have been times you were suspicious of Anthony's habits and actions" "No, I wasn't."

I asked what Anthony's relationship with Nathaniel was like.

"They're brothers," she said.

"Do they hang out together?"

"Yes, but not that often," she said. "Anthony and I live in Toledo and Nathaniel lives in Columbus."

I thanked her, saying I wanted to talk with Nathaniel, and would she mind waiting in the lobby? She said she would.

I felt Peggy Cook knew more than she was willing to admit, but I also believed she was probably more a victim of lies and a bad marriage than anything else.

Nathaniel Cook had his invisible body armor on when he took his turn in the interviewing room, and I felt sure he had prepared himself for a barrage of questions. I cordially greeted him like I would a victim or witness – a professional interrogator knows that you catch more bees with honey than you do with vinegar.

Nathaniel was apprehensive and cautious in his demeanor. Small talk was initiated.

"Hi, Moby, how are you?"

"Fine," he replied.

"Are you living in Toledo or are you still living in Columbus?"

"Columbus," he said.

"Are you working?"

"I drive a truck for Madison Brothers Trucking on Indiana Avenue, here in Toledo."

"What kind of trucks do you drive? What do you haul?"

He said he drove semis and hauled mostly steel to destinations in Ohio, Michigan and Indiana. I asked the usual questions about whether he was married or had kids. He wasn't and didn't. Nathaniel said he dated Nita Zeigler and that her father operated some type of group home in Toledo. He also said he used to travel back and forth to Diamond Bar, California, to see an old girlfriend, Benita Grey.

"Have you ever been in trouble with the police?"

"Not really," he said. "I got picked up for drugs once but they dropped the charges."

"Weren't you once arrested for arson in Columbus, Ohio?

"Yes, but I only spent a couple of days in jail before being acquitted."

"Tell me about those charges."

"No, I don't want to talk about it."

When checking Nathaniel's record, I discovered both the drug misdemeanor charge in Toledo and the arson charge in Columbus. I could find no other information about these charges, no reports or case dispositions. The charges must have been dismissed soon after the arrests. The drug arrest was on March 21, 1980, and the arson charge was in 1977.

"Do you use drugs often, Moby?"

"No," he replied, "just once in awhile." He said he used marijuana and he liked to drink now and then. He said he wasn't an addict who needed help.

"You know, Moby, I'm investigating numerous homicides in the Toledo area that have occurred over the last several years, and your brother Anthony has been arrested. The Sawicki murder is the last murder, but by far not the only murder Anthony is involved in. You know, Moby, some of the murders I'm investigating were committed by two killers. You and Anthony are tight, almost inseparable, I've

144

been told. I know you're involved in some of those homicides. I know the homicides were not your idea and that you only became involved because Anthony wanted you to. You have a conscience, Moby. I bet on occasions you probably even tried to talk Anthony into quitting.

"Moby, tell me about it, get it off your chest. I know it bothers you, it's eating you up inside."

For a moment I thought I'd broken through the body armor, but then Nathaniel caught himself and said he wasn't involved.

"Then tell me what you know about the murders. Who was with Anthony if not you?"

"I don't know," he said. "I can't help you."

"Did you and Anthony ever strip vacant houses and buildings of copper and other things to sell?"

He said they had stripped vacant houses and buildings in the inner city and sold the copper and other items at Tuschman Steel on Hill Avenue.

"Did you and Anthony ever strip the old State Theater on Collingwood by Scott High School, and sell the copper to Tuschman Steel Industries?"

" No, never was in there," he said.

I told Nathaniel we had witnesses placing him and Anthony in the State Theater stripping the building of copper, then selling it. We had the records from Tuschman Steel Industries showing they sold the metals there.

Moby still denied being in the State Theater, but did admit selling metals to Tuschman Steel from other vacant buildings. He obviously knew that by admitting he had been in the State Theater, we would believe he was involved in murdering Dawn Backes.

There is a fine line an investigator has to walk when interrogating a suspect. He has to know when to push a suspect and when to back off. I knew Nathaniel was nearing the point where he would quit cooperating and leave.

"Look, Moby, prove to me that you are not involved in any of these homicides.

Take a polygraph examination; give me fingerprints and hair samples. We have hairs and fingerprints found at the scenes. Give me yours and let's clear this up once and for all."

"I will, I will, Stiles," he said. "But I can't do it today, I'll come back."

I knew he wouldn't come back and, indeed, that this would be the last time we'd see him unless and until we had sufficient evidence to arrest him. Although we had no fingerprints of value and that the hair samples we had were not sufficient to make identification, I felt if Nathaniel provided the samples and took the polygraph; it might be enough to push him closer to a confession.

I had no choice but to allow him to go. As he left, he kept promising to return for the test but, of course, he never did.

When Nathaniel quit cooperating, I knew we had to concentrate on Anthony Cook, get him convicted, then, resume the investigation of the younger brother.

We had arrested the main killer and it was important to do everything in our power to make sure he was convicted so he could harm no one else. I felt that Nathaniel was a follower and would most likely do nothing without his brother leading him.

There would be another day when Nathaniel would answer for following his brother's fiendish lead.

Chapter 23

The Trial

W hat would become perhaps the most prominent criminal trial in Toledo history started Monday, March 2, 1982, before the Honorable Judge Reno Riley Jr. The trial of Anthony Cook for the aggravated murder of real estate developer Peter Sawicki, the attempted murders of his daughter, Leslie Sawicki, and her boyfriend, Todd Sabo, and the robbery of Todd and the attempted rape of Leslie, was to begin this day. Standing room only was the scene when jury selection commenced. Tight security engulfed the courtroom and courthouse as metal detectors were used to scrutinize spectators and witnesses.

The defense attorney team was made up of lead attorney Terrence Jones and counsel Charles Andrews and Ronnie Wingate.

Jones was a well-known and flamboyant defense attorney, a bright young man who fought for the rights of those he defended. His mind was sharp and he could voir dire a potential jury like no other attorney. Voir dire is a French phrase meaning "to speak the truth." Prosecutors and defense attorneys, as well as the presiding judge, have the opportunity during voir dire to conduct a preliminary examination of potential jurors in an attempt to determine if they are qualified, suitable, and competent to serve.

When Jones questioned a potential juror, he remembered everything that was said. He remembered their names, businesses, and backgrounds. While going from juror to juror, he addressed them by their names and quoted almost verbatim what the prosecutors had asked them during their voir dire, and what they had told the prosecutors. He did all this without taking a note or referring to notes.

Jones was impressive and commanded respect and attention.

Less than two years later, however, in February, 1984, Jones would be arrested for two counts of aggravated trafficking in drugs and two counts of drug abuse.

Jones defended himself at trial and won the two trafficking charges, but the jury convicted him of the two felony counts of drug abuse.

Visiting Judge Lyle Castle sentenced Jones to a year in jail and he was indefinitely suspended from practicing law by the Ohio Supreme Court.

After serving his time, Jones was released from the Marion Correctional Facility in February, 1987. He was employed in various jobs after his release and resided for a time in California, performing research for a law firm.

Jones returned to Toledo, and on October 24, 2000, the Ohio Supreme Court ruled to return Jones' license to practice law. Exactly one month after being reinstated to the bar, he died of heart failure on Nov. 24, 2000, having never practiced law again.

It appeared at times that Jones didn't know how to separate his professional life from his personal life. Sometimes he associated with those he defended and apparently was attracted to their lifestyle. This association led to drugs and disrespect. After he died, many agreed that his talents may have been wasted on his personal failures.

But during the years Jones practiced law, he was a formidable defense attorney – prosecutors knew trials with him would be difficult, and that they would have to be prepared.

I had many trials with Jones and had always been successful. He once asked me what my Zodiac sign was. When I said Virgo, he said, "I knew it, I knew it; you are so organized, thorough, methodical, and analytical." We had a mutual respect for one another professionally, while sometimes I couldn't accept Terry Jones' personal lifestyle, and – many times – poor courtroom demeanor, but maybe that was to be expected since we were invariably on opposite sides of the justice system.

In any case, I remember thinking what a shame it was that he allowed himself to become involved with drugs when he had so much to offer.

* * * * *

The prosecution consisted of Chief Lucas County Prosecutor Curtis E. Posner and Assistant Prosecutor George Runner. Posner was a straightforward, by-the-book prosecutor. He sorted fact from possibility, and when the evidence presented itself he gave the case his all, prosecuting to the fullest extent of the law. He didn't believe much in plea bargaining with the exception of first offenders and cases of a less serious nature. When he did plea bargain, he gave the defense attorney one chance, and if the deal was turned down, it was "See you in court!" When the trial began, Posner was prepared and it was full speed ahead.

Anthony Cook sat beside attorney Jones dressed in a suit and tie. He was neat in appearance, and if one didn't know he was the defendant, he might have been mistaken for an associate of his defense attorney. But I knew that behind his disguise was a serial killer who would just as soon torture and kill as to look at you. I remember wondering what he was thinking. Perhaps it was, "If I'd left no witnesses, I wouldn't be here today. If I beat this thing, I'll never leave another witness."

The prosecutors and defense attorneys took their turns questioning potential jurors. Each side only has six peremptory challenges, so they wanted to make sure they selected jurors they felt would be fair to their case.

"What is your name and occupation?" the attorneys asked. "Have you ever been arrested or has anyone in your family been arrested?" "Are you friends with or have you been friends with a police officer, defense attorney, or prosecutor?"

"Have you, a family member, or friend ever been the victim of a crime?" "Will you be able to listen to all the testimony and judge the truthfulness of all the witnesses, whether they are police officers, prosecution witnesses, or friends of the accused and defense witnesses?"

After the prosecutors and defense attorneys used all their challenges, a jury of seven men and five women were selected. The first phase of the trial began with opening statements. The prosecution remarked in opening statements that Anthony Cook was a killer, robber and rapist, who murdered Peter Sawicki when his criminal misdeeds went awry and Mr. Sawicki was summoned by his daughter, Leslie, for help.

The defense raised the issue of self defense, suggesting Cook may have been defending himself after he was overpowered by the victims and Peter Sawicki, who came to his daughter's defense. Jones stated that after Peter Sawicki arrived on the scene, he began beating Cook; that Peter wanted to kill Cook for attacking his daughter.

Posner drew a picture of how Todd and Leslie had been out for the evening at a South Toledo bar before heading home in Todd's van. While Todd was taking Leslie to her Ottawa Hills home, they decided to stop in the parking lot at her father's apartment complex.

Posner continued that after they talked for awhile in the van, Todd got out of the van. It was then that he and Leslie were accosted by Cook, armed with a pistol.

Cook forced them back into the van where he demanded money and Todd gave him $5. Cook had Leslie tie Todd's hands with electrical cord he got from a tool box in the van. Cook bound Leslie's hands and made her lie down in the van. He removed her slacks and started undoing his own pants, but before he could assault Leslie, Todd broke free and jumped Cook. During the ensuing struggle Todd forced the gun from Cook and held him at gunpoint. Leslie ran partially nude to the adjacent apartment building where she summoned police and her father.

Peter Sawicki arrived on the scene before the police. During the struggle that followed, Cook retrieved the gun and shot both Todd and Peter. Peter Sawicki died; Todd survived.

* * * * *

The first witness in the case was Daniel Betz, who lived in one of the nearby apartments. He testified that when he arrived home on the morning of the murder he saw a black man standing in the doorway of the laundry room, which was directly across from his basement apartment. He said he noticed that none of the washers or dryers were running nor did the man have any laundry. Betz said he didn't recognize the man as a tenant of the apartments and that he looked directly at the man for about 10 to 15 seconds before entering his own apartment. Betz positively identified Cook as the man he had seen and described.

* * * * *

The next witness, Marlene Doener, a resident of Terrace View South, said she was in her bedroom reading on the morning of the murder when she heard noises outside the apartment building. A few minutes later she heard what sounded like firecrackers or gunshots. She pulled the drapes back, looked out her window, and saw a light-colored car leaving the parking lot. Doener said she ran to the entrance door of the apartment building. A young lady was yelling, "He tried to rape me and he shot my father!"

Doener said she heard the young woman pleading and crying, 'Dad, please don't die!" She could see the silhouette of the young woman bending over the darkened figure of a man, pleading for her father not to die.

* * * * *

Prosecution witness Howard Lester testified he was at home in his apartment, around 20 minutes after midnight when he heard screaming and yelling. He looked out his window and saw a man drive up to where a van was parked. The man got out of his car and disappeared behind the van. He heard a loud commotion in the van and was going to call the police when five gunshots rang out. Lester testified he then called police and remained on the line as he watched a light-colored car race from the parking lot. He said no sooner had the car exited the lot when a Toledo police car arrived on the scene.

* * * * *

Kimberly Streets lived in the apartment building where Leslie Sawicki fled for help. She testified that after hearing pounding on her door, she opened it to find a horrified and screaming Leslie. The young woman said she had been assaulted and needed to call police. Streets said Leslie used her telephone to call the Ottawa Hills Police Department and screamed, "You have to send the police here right now! A man tried to rape me and the man has a gun. Send someone right away!"

Streets testified that Leslie was nude from the waist down, so she gave her a pair of jeans to put on. They both then peered out of her window watching for the police. Streets said Leslie became very upset that the Ottawa Hills police had not yet arrived, so she called her father. Leslie went back to the phone and again called the Ottawa Hills Police.

Streets said that Leslie then ran from the building toward where the men were yelling and struggling. As she crossed the parking lot, five or six shots rang out in rapid succession.

* * * * *

Toledo Policeman Harry Thoman took the stand next. He said he was one of the first officers to arrive. He administered first aid to Peter Sawicki and Todd Sabo while attempting to comfort them until emergency medics arrived.

* * * * *

Leslie Sawicki testified the following day. It was difficult for her to keep her composure while fighting back tears trickling down her face. She loved her father, he had always protected her, and he was her hero.

With her fist clenched, feet tapping and a strained look on her face, Leslie struggled to recount the events of the worst night of her life.

She and Todd had been out on a date that night when they decided to stop and talk in the parking lot at her father's apartment complex. They had parked there before because they felt safe knowing her father owned the apartments. Her grandmother lived in one of the apartments and she visited her often.

Leslie testified that, after some time passed, Todd stepped outside the van and was standing by the door when confronted by a man with a gun. She screamed as the man forced Todd back into the van. The gunman followed and asked them if they had any money. Todd said they didn't, but the gunman said he was lying. Leslie reminded Todd that she had given him $5 earlier while they were at a South End nightclub. Cook took the $5.

Leslie continued that the robber asked them personal questions such as where they lived and how they met each other. He then asked Todd what was in his toolbox. Todd said just some tools. The robber searched through the toolbox, taking some stereo speaker wire out of it. He made Leslie tie Todd's hands with the wire but after checking it the robber tied Todd's hands tighter.

Leslie testified that the robber then told Leslie to get into the back of the van. He tied her hands then made her lie on the floor of the van. The gunman pulled her slacks off and started undoing his own pants when Todd pleaded with him not to rape Leslie. The robber continued taking off his trousers when Leslie broke free of her bonds and started hitting and scratching the gunman.

Todd was so upset that with all his strength he broke free of the wires that bond his hands. Todd grabbed the gun hand of the robber. Leslie joined in the struggle and they were able to overpower the robber-would-be rapist and Todd got the gun.

Todd told Leslie to run and get help. She fled the van with only her top on. She ran to the adjacent apartments where her grandmother resided. She pounded on her grandmother's door but she didn't respond. She raced from apartment door to apartment door pounding on the doors and screaming for help. Finally, Kimberly Streets opened her door a crack and Leslie told her that a man had attempted to rape her and had a gun. Streets allowed her into her apartment and she called the Ottawa Hills Police Department.

Prosecutor Posner asked Leslie if she saw, in the courtroom, the person who assaulted them. Leslie pointed directly at Cook and told the jury, "He is the man who robbed us, tried to rape me and shot Todd and my father."

Leslie continued "I called the Ottawa Hills Police from Ms. Streets apartment and she gave me a pair of jeans to put on." Leslie went to the window and looked out into the parking lot. She became upset because the police still hadn't arrived. She thought, "Where are they," the Ottawa Hills Police Department is almost next door, just over the Toledo city limits line.

She called her father, who said, " Leslie, stay in the apartment, I am on the way."

Leslie said, when he arrived, she approached him and saw he was holding the robber's arms. Peter said, "He tried to rape you?" And she said yes. Todd had the robber's gun and after looking at it he threw it onto the grass. She said he apparently thought the gun was unloaded or he would not have thrown it away.

She watched in horror, fearing Todd and her father were in danger. Her father said, "I'm so upset I feel like killing him." She pleaded with her father not to. Peter Sawicki said to Leslie, "Do you want to hit him?" Leslie kicked the robber once in the shoulder area, but was barefooted and didn't think she hurt him.

The police still hadn't arrived when Peter Sawicki told his daughter to go for help again. As she turned and ran across the parking lot, back toward the apartment building, she heard gunshots. She hesitated momentarily then turned to see what was happening. She saw the gunman running towards her, then saw flames explode from the barrel of the gun the robber was holding.

She stumbled as she raced for the door to the apartment building. Out of breath, she slammed the door behind her thinking, "Oh, my God, I made it." She looked out the small window in the apartment building door just in time to see the white car leaving the parking lot. The car had no sooner exited the lot when Toledo Police arrived.

Leslie was shown the weapon I recovered from Cook's friend's yard and she said, that was the same gun, with the dirty white handle grips, that she saw Cook hold when he assaulted them.

* * * * *

A calm Todd Sabo took the witness stand and was sworn in. He confirmed what Leslie had testified to. He and Leslie had been to Renee's Nite Club in South Toledo. On their way to Leslie's house, they stopped in the parking lot at Terrace View North to talk for awhile. He had a few beers earlier and needed to urinate so he stepped from the van to the parking lot. Leslie got out too, he said, and that was when they were approached by a man armed with a revolver.

Prosecutor George Runner asked Todd if he saw the man in the courtroom, and Todd pointed to Cook.

Todd said, "I was going to let him rob me and thought he would then leave." Instead, Cook ordered them back into the van. Once inside, Cook stole $5 from Todd, then took some wire from his toolbox and made Leslie tie Todd's hands. Cook then took Todd's belt and tied Todd's feet together. Cook took Leslie to the rear of the van and tied her hands. An old shirt of Todd's was taken from the floor of the van by Cook and he tore it into strips.

He used the strips to gag Leslie. He took her slacks off and started pulling his pants down. Todd pleaded with Cook not to rape his girlfriend but Cook continued.

Leslie managed to untie herself, then struggled with Cook, fighting with all her strength. During their struggle, Todd said he managed to break free of his bonds. He jumped Cook and he and Leslie fought with Cook. Todd explained he managed to work the gun free from Cook's hand and took possession of it. He pointed the gun at Cook and Cook pleaded with Todd not to shoot him. Cook said that he had a wife and child and didn't want to die or go to jail.

Todd stated he told Leslie to go for help and she fled the van. After a long period of time that seemed like hours rather than minutes, Peter Sawicki arrived. They dragged Cook from the van to the ground and the struggle continued. Todd looked into the barrel of the gun while sitting on top of Cook and holding him down. He said he didn't see any bullets and thought the gun was unloaded.

Todd tossed the gun onto the nearby grass while still holding Cook for the police. As Todd looked up, he saw that Leslie had returned, but the police were still not there.

Leslie ran to summon help again and, suddenly, Todd heard a bang. Todd felt pain in his neck as a bullet pierced his flesh. Another shot rang out and he felt a sharp pain in his back. Other shots exploded and Peter Sawicki laid nearby, gasping for air. Todd struggled to look toward Peter and saw him bleeding but didn't have the strength to help him.

* * * * *

Peter Sawicki's widow, Marsha Sawicki, next took the stand. She said her husband had been in bed and was dressed in his pajamas when the telephone rang. She said she heard Peter say "I'll be right there," and he frantically left the house.

When asked if Peter had a gun with him when he left, Marsha said no, he owned only one handgun and it was found in the house after his death.

Marsha described both the physical and mental injuries Leslie suffered as a result of the attack.

She said Todd not only dated Leslie but had worked for her husband in the summer doing odd jobs. "He is a nice young man," Marsha said.

* * * * *

Dr. Renate Fazekas, assistant coroner, testified that Peter Sawicki died of a gunshot wound through the neck which continued into his left shoulder. "There was no evidence of close-range firing on the skin surrounding the entrance wound," Fazekas said. A small-caliber, non-jacketed lead slug was recovered and kept for evidence. Peter also had a graze gunshot wound to the left upper arm.

* * * * *

Crime Scene Technician Larry Mallory, assigned to the Toledo Police Scientific Investigation Unit, described how he processed the crime scene and collected evidence. He identified the wire used to tie Leslie and Todd's hands, the belt used to tie Todd's feet, and strips of an old shirt taken from Todd's van and used to gag Leslie, as items found in the parking lot where the van was parked. Todd and Leslie identified these items, during their testimony, as the ones used to tie their hands and feet and to gag Leslie.

Mallory displayed photographs he had taken of the crime scene and sketches he had made to scale of the area. Through the photographs and sketches the jury was able to visualize where and what had taken place on the night of the murder and assaults. When asked if any drugs were found he indicated none had been found.

* * * * *

Cook's close friend, Ernest Kynard, testified that Cook confessed to the murder of Peter Sawicki and the assaults on Leslie and Todd. When Kynard testified, it was as if he had just heard the testimony of Leslie and Todd. The story he unfolded was an echo of what Todd and Leslie had testified to.

Kynard testified to what he had told me during our interview. Cook came to his apartment the morning following Sawicki's murder. He told him about the robbery, shooting of Todd Sabo, murder of Peter Sawicki, and attempted rape of Leslie.

Kynard testified that Cook told him he wished he had a rifle with a scope on it so he could track Leslie Sawicki down and kill her. He felt the men had died and that she was the only one who could identify him. Kynard said, "Tony, you're crazy." He told Cook to get rid of the gun but Cook talked him into hiding the gun in his yard. Cook also left a box of .22 shells with him and he hid those in his apartment. He said when he was questioned by Stiles he showed him where the gun and bullets were hidden.

On cross examination by defense attorney Jones, as well as on redirect by prosecutor Runner, Kynard said he gave a taped statement to Sgt. Stiles because he was afraid he would be arrested for complicity to commit murder and withholding evidence.

* * * * *

Doctor Willard Emch, the neurologist who treated Todd Sabo for the wounds to his head and neck, testified about Todd's injuries. He said if the bullet had taken a slightly different direction, the injuries could have been fatal.

* * * * *

The 15th and final witness for the prosecution was me, the lead detective in the case. I had been in the courtroom throughout the trial because the lead detective is allowed to sit at the prosecution's table to assist.

I testified about my informant, who gave me information that led to Kynard. My informant only knew Kynard by his nickname of "Mayne," but I found out his real name when interviewing neighbors and witnesses.

During my interview with Kynard I discovered Cook's involvement in the murder of Peter Sawicki and the assaults on Leslie Sawicki and Todd Sabo. Kynard showed me where he and Cook hid the gun.

After recovering the murder weapon and building a case against Cook, I obtained arrest warrants for Cook charging him with the aggravated murder of Peter Sawicki, attempted murder and robbery of Todd Sabo, and the attempted rape of Leslie Sawicki. I also took search warrant affidavits I prepared to Judge Robert Christiansen who authorized search warrants for Cooks house, his truck and his wife's car, which Cook used in the Sawicki and Sabo crimes.

We arrested Cook on Oct. 14, at 10:30 p.m. while he was driving his green and white pickup truck on Interstate 475 at Interstate 75. He had no gun nor did he resist.

During my interrogation of Anthony Cook, he didn't make a full confession, but he never denied the crimes. Cook admitted that he thought he looked like the police artist drawing of Sawicki's murderer, and when asked where he was on the morning Sawicki and Sabo were shot, Cook said he had no alibi. Before the interrogation could be continued, an attorney hired by Cook's family interrupted. When attorney Alan Kirshner appeared on behalf of his client, and Cook requested to speak with him, I had to cease the interrogation .

I continued that, immediately after questioning Cook and booking him in the Lucas County Jail, we executed the search warrants for Cook's truck, his wife's car, and his house. Assorted clothing matching the description of clothing worn during the assaults was confiscated with the search warrants.

I testified about conducting a lineup with Cook at the Lucas County Jail after his arrest. Both Leslie and Todd quickly identified their assailant as Anthony Cook.

I was the final prosecution witness and I tied the case up by summarizing the facts of the investigation and the compelling evidence.

The prosecution rested its case after all the exhibits, including the gun, clothing, sketches and photographs of the crime scene were admitted into evidence by Judge Riley.

* * * * *

Much to the surprise of many, Anthony Cook took the witness stand in his own defense.

Cook testified that the whole thing was a drug deal. Todd Sabo was to sell him cocaine, and Kynard put him up to the drug buy. He said he was to purchase $300 worth of cocaine for Kynard. Cook pulled into the parking lot, parked his car, and walked up to Todd Sabo's van. He said he saw Leslie Sawicki urinating and Sabo got mad because he had witnessed her in a compromising position. Cook said that Sabo became more upset when he found out that Cook didn't have sufficient money to pay for the quantity of cocaine Sabo had for sale.

Cook said the conversation continued inside Todd's van where

Sabo jumped him. He said while they fought, Leslie Sawicki left the van. Five minutes later a car pulled up and Peter Sawicki entered the van. He said both Sawicki and Sabo started attacking him. Cook said Peter Sawicki had a gun and he was the only one who had a gun.

Cook continued that he was pulled from the van by Sabo and Sawicki while Sawicki was pointing the gun at him. He said Sabo was on top of him when Sawicki told Sabo to move out of his way. As Sabo got up to move out of the way, Cook said he grabbed the gun and struggled with Sawicki. During the struggle, he heard the gun go off. He said he then fired the gun until it was empty.

Cook admitted during cross examination by Prosecutor Posner that he had been convicted for robberies in the past involving weapons and he had served six years in prison for the last robbery. He said he was released in 1979.

Also during direct examination, Cook testified that he destroyed the gun Sawicki allegedly brought to the scene. He said he destroyed the gun with a cutting torch a few days after the shootings.

During cross examination, Posner held up the .22 caliber revolver in evidence and which both Leslie Sawicki and Todd Sabo had testified was the gun Cook used to rob them and to shoot Todd and Peter Sawicki.

Posner asked Cook, "Did you see this gun on the morning of Sept. 18, 1981, when Peter Sawicki was killed?"

Cook: "Did I see that gun?"

Posner: "Yes."

Cook replied yes.

Posner: "Where did you see it at?"

Cook: "In my car."

Posner repeated what Cook had said, "You saw it in your car."

"Yes," Cook said.

Posner asked what the gun was doing in his car. Cook answered, "Well, I had shot Sawicki."

You could hear a pin drop in the packed courtroom. The audience was shocked that Cook had just admitted that the gun in evidence was in fact the gun he had shot Peter Sawicki and Todd Sabo with. To everyone's disbelief, Cook had just admitted to the shootings with a gun he brought to the scene.

Posner pointed out to Cook that he had testified earlier that he had destroyed the gun used in the shootings.

Cook seemed to get control of himself again and said that he was under the impression that his attorney, Jones, had asked him about a gun that he had prior to the day of the Sawicki and Sabo shootings.

To support the fact that the gun in evidence was the gun used to murder Sawicki and to injure Sabo, witness Kynard had testified about Cook's confession to him, that he had shot both Sabo and Sawicki and then hid the gun at his apartment. The gun was recovered at Kynard's after the shootings and Cook identified the gun in court, as did Leslie Sawicki and Todd Sabo.

I thought how clever it was for the prosecutor to seize on the obvious inconsistency.

* * * * *

Jones, visibly shaken by Cook's testimony and admissions, also called to the stand a few Toledo police officers who had been at the crime scene and interviewed some of the witnesses and victims. He pointed out small discrepancies between what the witnesses and victims had testified to and what the officers had documented in their reports. Jones was trying to create belief among the jurors that the witnesses, victims, and perhaps the police had lied. The discrepancies were so small and insignificant that his ploy to discredit didn't work.

* * * * *

During closing arguments, Posner summarized the state's case, pointing out that both Todd Sabo and Leslie Sawicki identified Cook as their assailant. He continued that the evidence supported all five counts of the indictments.

Testimony was that Todd and Leslie were robbed of $5; Cook had tried to rape Leslie by taking her slacks off and partially removing his own before Todd broke his bonds and overpowered Cook.

Posner pointed out that Leslie ran for help and summoned police along with her father, Peter Sawicki. Cook got his gun back during the struggle with Sabo and Sawicki then shot and killed Sawicki while seriously injuring Sabo.

Cook shot at Leslie Sawicki but missed, then fled the scene.

Posner further pointed out that Cook first said the gun was brought to the Crime scene by Sawicki and that after the shooting he destroyed the gun by cutting it up with a torch. He later admitted during questioning by Posner that he had his own gun in his car and used it to shoot Sawicki and Sabo.

Posner told the jury that if there is to be justice, not only to the defendant but for the citizens of Lucas County, their verdict must be guilty on all five counts of the indictment.

Jones contended that Cook had gone to the parking lot to purchase cocaine from Todd Sabo, who became angry when Cook didn't have enough money to purchase the drugs, and he was also upset about Cook seeing Leslie urinating. Jones indicated the prosecution brought the rape charge in an attempt to draw sympathy toward Leslie Sawicki. He further indicated that the prosecution's case was built on lies.

He downplayed what Cook said about the gun and passed it off as just a mistake on the part of his client. He said if Cook was lying about the gun, he could have made up a better story. He pointed out that the ballistics test done on the gun could not establish beyond a reasonable doubt that the gun was used in the shootings.

Jones told the jury members that the state did not prove its case beyond a reasonable doubt, so they must come back with a finding of not guilty.

* * * * *

At the end of the 11-day trial and after almost five hours of closing arguments, the jury was given the case. The jurors sought seclusion in the jury room to begin their deliberation. They deliberated five hours before they were retired after midnight by Judge Riley. Due to the seriousness of the charges and the notoriety of the case, the jurors were sequestered and secured in hotel rooms for the night.

After a short Friday night the jurors resumed their deliberation at 10 a.m. Saturday. They deliberated seven hours before reaching a verdict.

The jury had deliberated a total of 12 hours before reaching their unanimous verdict. The trial had lasted 11 exhausting days.

* * * * *

The courtroom was packed with spectators and security when the foreman of the jury read the verdict.

"On the charge of aggravated murder, we find the defendant not guilty but guilty to the lesser charge of murder. We find the defendant guilty to attempted murder of Leslie Sawicki, we find the defendant guilty of attempted murder of Todd Sabo, we find the defendant guilty to aggravated robbery, and we find the defendant guilty to the attempted rape of Leslie Sawicki."

Many in the courtroom couldn't understand why the jurors found Cook guilty to the lesser charge of murder, but jurors have their own way of reasoning.

Jones requested that the jurors be polled after the verdict was read. One by one, each juror was asked if this was their verdict. One by one, they each said, "Yes, it is my verdict."

Judge Riley sentenced Cook on March 18, 1982, to the longest term he could under state law for the five convictions. Cook was sentenced to imprisonment for 15 years to life for murder; five to 25 years for each of the attempted murders; five to 25 years for the aggravated robbery; and five to 25 years for the attempted rape, all to be served concurrently with the sentence for murder, but consecutively with each other. Cook would most likely spend the rest of his life in prison.

Cook himself stood stone-faced as the judge passed sentence. He chose not to make a statement, and showed no remorse or emotion.

The remaining indictments against Cook – aggravated robbery of Charles Hackenberg and Laurie Specht while they sat in Charles' car on July 23, 1981, and the attempted abduction of Janie Fall while she walked home from work on June 22, 1981 – were dismissed by the court. Under Ohio law, Cook could not be given any additional prison time should he be convicted in those cases.

The prosecutor's office voiced its frustration with the multiple sentencing statutes that prevented the judge from imposing a minimum prison term of more than 20 years in prison. Under this condition, it was pointless to take the other cases to trial and to expose the victims to the ordeal. Cook received the maximum sentence he could get.

Was it enough? A lot of people who knew about Anthony Cook didn't think so.

Lucas County Prosecutor Curtis E. Posner

Defense Attorney Terrence Jones

In the courtroom – Front row – from left to right – Anthony Cook,
Attorney Terrence Jones, and Sgt. Frank Stiles

Victim Leslie Sawicki testifying

Victim Todd Sabo, while testifying, points to where he was shot by
Anthony Cook.

Victim Todd Sabo using police drawing to show where crime occurred.

Marsha Sawicki testifying

Chapter 24

After the trial

The trial was the center of conversation – not only among law enforcement and the legal community, but from the citizens of Lucas County.

The two-week trial dominated the newspaper and TV every night. The excitement of the trial was the main topic of many family and friends' get-togethers. A barber said to his customer, while cutting his hair, "Can you believe there are people like Anthony Cook out there? Do you think he killed all those kids? I hope he's the one. I have a 19-year-old daughter."

The murders descended like a plague on the Toledo area for the last two years. People were scared to go out alone at night and parents were afraid for their teenage children. After Cook's conviction, a calm fell over the city and county.

The total number of homicides in Toledo in 1980 was 60; in 1981 there were 55 homicides and in 1982 there were 27. After we arrested Cook for the Sawicki murder, the homicides decreased 51 percent for the following year. Even though Anthony Cook was only convicted for the Peter Sawicki murder, one had to wonder why the homicides fell so dramatically the year following his arrest. Most importantly, the type of killings Cook was arrested for and suspected of stopped immediately after his arrest.

I felt pride and a sense of victory for myself, the prosecutors, and all the other dedicated detectives and police officers who had worked on the homicides.

But, I also knew from the evidence we had accumulated and the witnesses we had interviewed during all the investigations that there was much work to be done. I felt I couldn't rest until all the homicides were cleared and the second killer was caught. I knew in my mind that the second murderer was Tony Cook's brother, Nathaniel.

As soon as the trial was over, I prepared a list of all the homicides and crimes I felt Anthony Cook or his brother may have committed. I'd been putting this list together as the homicides unfolded over the last two years. I evaluated all the evidence that had been accumulated and used the information, as well as the modus operandi used by the killers, to create the list.

The list included all the victims and crimes I investigated during this series of kidnappings, robberies, rapes, attempted and actual murders.

The victims were white, and all the young women appeared to have been raped. Most of the women had been made to redress after they were raped and before they were murdered. The obvious assumption was that the killer or killers were trying to hide the fact that the victim had been raped, while the redressing may also have represented a sort of twisted guilt associated with the rapes.

Most of the victims died after being tortured. I tied Anthony and/or Nathaniel to all the areas where the crimes occurred. I knew from the friends and relatives I interviewed that Anthony had a hatred for whites, and I knew he liked rough sex. The 22-caliber pistol that belonged to Anthony, and which was recovered at his friend Ernest Kynard's home, had similar ballistic characteristics as the gun used in several of the homicides.

All these facts added up and I had no doubt that the brothers were responsible for all or most of the crimes on my list.

From the date the trial ended, March 14, 1982, until I retired from the Toledo Police Division to take a full-time security directors job with Lion Stores, a retail store chain, on April 26, 1990, I followed every lead that came in on any of these cases. I went back through all the reports and evidence, interviewed new and past witnesses, and even drove to Lucasville Penitentiary in southern Ohio in 1983 to re-interview Anthony Cook.

As I drove south on Route 23 through southern Ohio for the April interview, I thought what beautiful country it was. It was the beginning of spring and the grass was turning deep green. I thought how awful it must be for Cook to be imprisoned in some institution, never being able to breathe fresh air and enjoy nature's unexplainable beauty.

There are two things in life I wouldn't want to live without, health and freedom. Why would anyone jeopardize his freedom by committing crimes, knowing he would be jailed and lose the meaning of life itself? What makes people like Anthony Cook rape, kill and torture other human beings? They must be harboring some deep hatred. Anthony Cook must have had a horrible childhood. For a moment, I almost felt sorry for him.

As I pulled up to the prison, the beauty of the countryside and peacefulness I enjoyed on the way ended abruptly. The prison stood out like a sore in the middle of the sprawling countryside, enclosed with double barb-wire fencing and separated by concertina razor wire.

There was razor wire on top of the fences as well as in between the two sections of fencing. It would not be a pretty sight if one attempted to escape through or over the fence.

I pulled into the parking area, located in front of the prison, and as I walked from my car to the heavily guarded reception center, I could understand why inmates became hardened and would sometimes lose hope.

I felt there was a small probability that Cook would even see me, and that is why I drove there unannounced. Inmates don't have to see anyone they don't want to see, but I wanted to catch Cook off guard in hopes he would not have time to think about it and refuse to see me. Maybe he'd agree out of curiosity – or just for a break in his numbing routine.

Surprisingly, Cook indeed agreed to see me. Before I could enter, I was searched by hand and with metal detectors. My gun and personal property were taken, then the long walk to where Cook waited. I walked through one sliding steel door after another.

There were no pretty painted walls or pictures, just barren gray steel corridors with sliding steel-bar doors. Finally, I was escorted into a small room and seated at a steel table with welded attached bench seats. Cook sat on one side and I sat on the other. It was like the night I arrested Cook for the Sawicki murder: We sat there face to face playing each other to find out what the other knew or had in mind.

"How are you, Tony?"

"Alright," he said.

"Are they treating you OK?"

"I get by."

"What do you do to pass the time?"

"I'm a mechanic and I work on the prison vehicles."

"That's right," I said. "You worked on the trucks you drove for O'Dell Edwards."

I wanted to build a rapport with Cook, hoping he would be honest in answering the tough questions I was about to ask. After all the small talk, I mentioned some of the thoughts I had on the way to the prison.

"Tony, there are always reasons why we do things, "I recall telling him. "You had a hard life, I know that. People who are underprivileged and mistreated sometimes strike out, they sometimes want others to feel their pain and suffer the way they have. A moment of hatred and resentment can overpower one's judgment and sometimes cause a person to do horrible things that they really didn't want to do."

I was just six inches from Cook's face when I said, "Tony, it's time to forget the hatred and make peace with yourself. You have done some very terrible things and it's time you release that hatred and make peace with yourself. I have been working on the crimes you have committed and I know what you have done."

I went through the list of homicides and crimes I believed Cook was responsible for and pointed out the evidence I felt implicated him.

"Tony, you can do something decent for the families of all those victims, you can give closure to them. By admitting what you have done, you can give the families, relatives, and friends of those victims peace of mind. Knowing who harmed their loved ones will bring peace to them, and it will help you bring peace to yourself."

I think there is a little good in even the worst, and I gave Cook that chance, too. I also felt, however, that Cook may be the exception to that rule.

"I'm even being blamed for murders I didn't do," Cook said. "They even think I murdered Cindy Anderson."

Cook said a reporter had called him just before I arrived and asked him if he murdered Cindy Anderson. Most of the time media people are an asset to the investigator, but sometimes they can hinder with their eagerness. Apparently, this reporter got wind that I was going to Lucasville to interview Cook and thought he would beat me to the punch.

Cindy Anderson was the young woman who had worked at a lawyer's office in North Toledo. She came up missing on Aug. 4, 1981 and has not been seen since.

The Cindy Anderson case was on my list of possibilities concerning the Cooks, but only slightly. Cindy did not fit Tony Cook's usual method because she vanished during the daytime – Cook had always stalked at night. She was either taken from the building she was working in or from the parking lot adjacent to the building, while the other victims on the list were abducted in their cars or while walking late at night on the street.

Really, one couldn't exclude all possibility that Cook was involved in the Anderson case. He lived in the area from which she came up missing – and it appears she met with tragedy. But a dead-on match to the other cases I suspected Cook was involved in? We couldn't say that.

"Tony," I said. "I don't want you to admit to anything you haven't done, but clear up the ones you have done. You can take pride in knowing you have done something worthwhile."

He looked at me and said, "Stiles, you know that if I admit any of those other murders that I would never have a chance of being paroled. I'll probably spend the rest of my life in prison, but there's always that little bit of hope that I will be released someday."

I knew Cook would probably die with his deadly secrets. I politely said goodbye and left.

Chapter 25

DNA (Deoxyribonucleic Acid)

When I retired from the Toledo Police Division on April 26, 1990, to start a new career as a security director, I took my list with me. I never forgot the other victims ... I couldn't.

Time passed, but I often thought about the unsolved cases. I still blamed myself for not doing a better job, thinking of the brutal ways in which those innocent young people had suffered.

One day in the middle of October, 1997, I received a telephone call from Julia Bates, the elected Lucas County prosecuting attorney. I had known her for many years while working police felony cases and while she was an active trial prosecutor. On Oct. 23, 1999, Julie's husband, Common Pleas Judge James Bates, married me and the woman I love, B.J. Stiles. Judge Bates and I had known each other for many years, too; he had handled several of my felony cases while he was a prosecutor.

Jim and Julie Bates met while both were employed by the county prosecutor's office. B.J. and I were married in a small family-and-friends ceremony by Judge Bates at the home of our good friends, George and Marianne Ballas. George was the owner of George Ballas Buick, a prominent car dealership in Toledo. George would later pass on and Marianne carries on the family business.

"Hi, Frank, how's it going?" Julie asked.

"Fine, Julie, it's nice to hear from you."

"Frank, you worked the Cook cases, right?"

"Yeah. I arrested Tony for the Sawicki murder but didn't have sufficient evidence to arrest his brother Nathaniel or to solve all the other murders I feel they committed."

"Frank, I attended a prosecutor's conference recently and during the meetings the Dr. Sam Sheppard case came up."

Sheppard was an osteopath who lived in Bay Village, Ohio, a suburb of Cleveland, with his wife, Marilyn, and their 6-year-old son, Sam Reese Sheppard. On July 4, 1954, while the family slept, Marilyn Sheppard, who was pregnant with her second child, was bludgeoned to death. Sam Sheppard was arrested and during a nationally publicized trial he was convicted.

Years passed before Sheppard won an appeal for a new trial. He was acquitted during the second trial, but there was always speculation about whether he was guilty. Many people felt he was guilty and nothing was going to change their minds. The case inspired a TV series and the successful 1990s film, "The Fugitive," with Harrison Ford as a wrongfully convicted doctor and Tommy Lee Jones as the U.S. Marshal who tried to capture him after his escape.

Sheppard's son grew up believing in his father's innocence and made every attempt to clear his name.

At the time of the murder, blood evidence was collected from the crime scene. Over 40 years later, and after DNA technology was discovered, the blood from the murder scene was tested with Sheppard's DNA and that of his wife's. The blood was found not to be Sheppard's or his wife's; rather, the DNA had the same characteristics of a man by the name of Richard Eberling. Eberling was incarcerated for a different murder at this time but it was found that he had worked as a window washer for the Sheppard's around the time Marilyn Sheppard was murdered.

After his father's death, young Sam Sheppard continued his battle to clear his father's name. Even though Sheppard's conviction had been overturned during the second trial, there were many who still felt he was guilty. The son filed a lawsuit against the State of Ohio claiming wrongful imprisonment.

Eberling never admitted to the murder of Marilyn Sheppard before he died, so Sheppard's son had to rely on the DNA testing to clear his father. However, at the conclusion of the civil trial, the jury ruled against the son's case, and he has never been able to clear his dad. It is not known why the jury ruled against the younger Sheppard's case, but perhaps it was because DNA use in trials was relatively new at the time, or public opinion was so strong that it tainted the juror's minds.

Julia said, "I was lying in bed the other night and thought to myself, if they can use DNA in the Sheppard case, then why can't we use it in the Cook cases?"

I said, "Julie that is a great idea. I can give you all the cases to look at and the report numbers of those cases, so you can pull the reports and get the property room numbers where the evidence in each case is being stored." Evidence in murder cases is never to be destroyed because there is no statutory limit for prosecuting murder cases.

I told Julia about my list of the murders I felt the Cook brothers had committed. I told her I would mail it to her so police investigators could reopen the cases. Even though I was no longer employed by the city, I would do anything possible to help bring the Cook brothers to justice.

As soon as I got home from work that evening, I found the list and mailed a copy to Julia. It was Oct 15, 1997.

Toledo police detective Tom Ross and Sgt. Steve Forrester were assigned to follow up on the DNA investigation. Tom had worked on some of the early murder investigations before I arrested Anthony Cook for the Peter Sawicki murder, so he was familiar with the murder series.

The detectives went through the list of unsolved rape/homicide cases that the Cook brothers were suspected of; looking for clothing that might contain DNA evidence.

Sergeant Keefe Snyder, director of the police Scientific Investigation Unit, and S.I.U. technician and police artist Terry Cousino, assisted the detectives by using an alternate ultraviolet light source. They examined the clothing of the homicide and rape victims, searching for semen and DNA evidence. The scientific experts found semen when searching the clothing of rape victim Sandra Podgorski. After the preliminary test showed positive for semen, the samples along with Ms. Podgorski's DNA sample were sent to the Medical College of Ohio laboratory for DNA testing.

Two individual DNA samples not matching the victims were found in the panties of victim Podgorski. Podgorski was a surviving victim but her boyfriend Thomas Gordon was shot to death during the assaults on the couple.

Now that the officers had the foreign DNA samples from Podgorski's panties, the next step was to get the DNA of the Cook brothers. Once their samples were obtained, all the samples could be compared.

Sergeant Forrester and Detective Ross were aware that I had held a line-up on Oct. 15, 1981, where Podgorski viewed suspect Anthony Cook, but they were not aware of the fact that I had also shown Podgorski a photo array with Nathaniel Cook's photo included. When Podgorski viewed the line-up of Anthony Cook, and was shown the photo array, she indicated that they could be the killers but did not make a positive identification.

On Feb. 11, 1998 the detectives showed Podgorski a photo array including the picture of Nathaniel Cook. This photo had a better profile view and this time Podgorski was able to positively identify Nathaniel as the killer who had raped her and who shot and killed her boyfriend.

Since Anthony Cook was still in prison for the Peter Sawicki murder, his DNA profile was on file with the Ohio Bureau of Criminal Identification and Investigation, our state crime laboratory. By law, there were certain criminal offenses a prisoner's DNA sample was automatically taken.

The samples are taken from the prisoner by swabbing the inside of the mouth with a Q-tip like swab called a "buccal-swab." Both sides of the mouth are swabbed with two different buccal-swabs, then packaged separately, taking extreme care not to contaminate the samples. The known samples are analyzed, classified and the individual's DNA profile is kept on file in a computer program known as "CODIS."

"CODIS" stands for "Combined DNA Index System." If DNA is discovered at a crime scene, that DNA can be furnished to our state crime laboratory. The laboratory technician will analyze the DNA and enter it into CODIS. If the profiling matches a suspect who has his DNA on file, the investigator who submitted the request is notified. If the match is conclusive, the suspect can be investigated and arrested.

There are 10 BCI Laboratories throughout the state of Ohio and they enter their DNA profiling data into a national electronic network once a week so all the DNA profiling taken from prisoners throughout the nation are in "CODIS." DNA profiling is sometimes called DNA fingerprinting.

DNA was discovered by 1962 Nobel Prize winning scientist, James Watson and Francis Crick as early as 1953, but was not used to identify individual donors until 1984 when Dr. Alec Jeffreys of Great Britain began comparing fragments of DNA from different subjects as a way to identify independent donors.

DNA profiling first became prominent in 1985 when Scotland Yard presented DNA evidence in the case of a rape defendant, Robert Melias, whose attorney pleaded him guilty after being confronted with the scientific explanation of the test results.

Based on the recent identification by Sandra Podgorski, detectives Ross and Forrester obtained an aggravated murder warrant for Nathaniel Cook and arrested him on Feb. 13, 1998. A search warrant was obtained to take a DNA sample from him, and this was done the same day of his arrest.

Anthony Cook's computerized DNA profile was compared with the DNA found in Podgorski's panties and the two matched. Based on the initial testing a search warrant was obtained to take blood from Anthony Cook for a second DNA testing. Anthony was brought back from Chillicothe Correctional Institute on March 9, 1998. His blood sample was taken and both his and Nathaniel's were sent to the Medical College of Ohio lab for DNA testing. The Cook brother's DNA was to be compared against the two individual DNA samples found in the panties of Podgorski. The testing came back positive for each brother.

Anthony and Nathaniel Cook were indicted by a Lucas County grand jury for three counts of aggravated murder. The counts included aggravated murder in the commission of a robbery, aggravated murder in the commission of kidnapping, and aggravated murder in the commission of rape.

Nathaniel Cook was indicted on Feb. 20, 1998, and Anthony Cook was indicted on May 29.

The Cook brothers were indicted on the three charges, but if found guilty, the law only permitted them to be sentenced for one count. The penalty for aggravated murder was punishable by life in prison with a possibility of parole after 20 years.

This was the maximum sentence that could be imposed by a judge under the laws of Ohio. The U.S. Supreme Court had ruled the death penalty unconstitutional during this period of time, so the prosecutor's couldn't use death specifications when the indictments were sought.

Prosecutor Bates hired me as her chief investigator on Jan. 25, 1999. Later that year Tom Ross retired from the Toledo Police Division and was hired as an investigator for the prosecutor's office. The two detectives who had spent so much time tracking the Cook brothers while with the Toledo Police were now part of the prosecutor's team.

After all the hearings and motions were exhausted, the smoke cleared and both defendants accepted a plea agreement. The agreements were worked out and agreed upon by attorneys for Anthony Cook; Jeffrey J. Helmick and Catherine G. Hoolahan, attorneys for Nathaniel Cook; Robert Z. Kaplan and Peter G. Rost, and prosecutors Julia R. Bates, Dean P. Mandross, and Timothy F. Braun.

Anthony Cook and his attorneys agreed that he would plead to the aggravated murder of Thomas Gordon. He agreed that he would make a statement in open court sufficient to acknowledge each and every essential element of the crime to which he was pleading guilty.

He further agreed to make a full and complete disclosure of any and all other homicides in Lucas County in which he had been involved, including statements as to the involvement of any other individuals in the crimes.

Tony agreed to take a polygraph examination, as to any statements he was to make regarding any of the homicides. Cook agreed that his failure to pass any polygraph examination would give the State the right to void the agreement, up to the time in which his sentence was imposed. It was further agreed that the court would impose the mandatory sentence of life imprisonment to be served consecutive to the life sentence in which he was presently serving for the Peter Sawicki murder.

In exchange for his commitments, the State agreed that it wouldn't prosecute him for any other homicides in Lucas County to which he made a full, complete and honest disclosure.

Nathaniel Cook and his attorneys agreed that Nathaniel would plead guilty to a bill of information charging him with attempted aggravated murder and two counts of kidnapping, all first-degree felonies. He agreed to waive any statute of limitations as to the charges in which he was pleading guilty to. He acknowledged that he understood that the court was going to sentence him to the maximum term on each count and make these sentences consecutive to one another for a total sentence of 21 to 75 years.

It was further agreed that Nathaniel Cook would be released from prison after serving 20 full years in prison. The rest of his agreements were the same as his brother's.

These agreements were made only after all the victims or their families agreed to the plea conditions. All concerned agreed it was important to know who murdered their loved ones and to bring closure.

Before the agreements were finalized, the Cook brothers had to confess their sins and admit to all the homicides and crimes they committed in Lucas County. No agreements could be made with the brothers as to any homicides and crimes they may have committed outside of Lucas County because the prosecutors didn't have jurisdiction over such cases. It was further agreed that if the Cook brothers neglected to admit any murders or crimes they committed in

Lucas County, they would be subject to prosecution for those offenses.

I thought to myself, the time had finally come. We now would be able to clear the cases I always knew the Cook brothers had committed. Arrangements were made for Anthony and Nathaniel Cook to be transported from the county jail to the district police substation on Monday, April 3, 2000 at, 9a.m.

It was here where they would give their confessions. If all went well, the official sentencing would take place on April 6, before Lucas County Common Pleas Court Judge Charles S. Wittenberg.

Former Toledo Police Department detectives Frank Stiles on the left and Thomas Ross on the right, investigators for the Lucas County Prosecutor's Office, display some of the accumulated homicide files involving Anthony and Nathaniel Cook.

Chapter 26

The Confessions

Tom Ross, Steve Forrester, and I met at the substation at 9 a.m. April 3, 2000, to take the long-awaited confessions from the Cook brothers. Tom and Steve had spoken briefly with the Cook brothers the night before – after the agreement had been made between the prosecutors and the defense attorneys. During that conversation we learned which homicides the Cook brothers would confess to.

Anthony Cook would be the first killer interviewed because he was in on all the murders, while Nathaniel participated in only a few of the murders and rapes. The confessions would be taped on audio and video. Tony Cook was led into a small interviewing room and the interview commenced at 9:45 a.m. I was in the room with Tom and Steve, representing the Lucas County Prosecutor's Office and the Toledo Police Division. Also present were Cook's attorneys, Jeffrey Helmick and Catherine Hoolahan.

For the purpose of the tape, everyone in the room was identified, and the time, date, and location of the interview were recorded.

Cook sat calmly in his chair, showing no emotion. I thought that had to be the hardest thing he ever did in his life. Telling about all the murders he had worked so hard to conceal must have been difficult and infuriating for him. All the terrible things he did to those innocent young people would now be made public.

Hesitantly, Cook described what he said was his very first murder. By the description of the events and people he described, the murder was that of 22-year-old Vicki Lynn Small.

Vicki and her girlfriend, Heather, had gone out for the evening on Dec. 19, 1973, in Heather's car. It was snowing heavily the following morning when returning home. They got stuck in the snow a short distance from Vicki's home.

Two black men in a Pontiac pulled up behind them and assisted them in getting out of the deep snow. The driver of the Pontiac suggested he drive Vicki home because his car was heavier and they would not get stuck. Vicki agreed but instead of arriving home safely she was later found in Ottawa Park, shot to death by someone with a .25-caliber pistol. Vicki had been beaten, raped, shot four times in the head, two times in the chest and dumped in the snow in Ottawa Park.

Cook did not remember being with anyone the night of the murder. He said he was in his tan Pontiac Catalina when he came upon the victim and her girlfriend stuck in the snow near the hospital off Cherry Street. It was in the winter around the year 1971, Cook said, but conceded that it could have been in 1973.

He said he was helping them push the car out of the snow when a man around 50 years old stopped behind them. Cook said the man couldn't get past because their cars were blocking the street. The man helped them push the car out of the snow, then left. The one girl was afraid to let her friend continue to drive her home for fear of getting stuck again, Cook said.

"I offered to give the woman a ride home and she accepted." He guessed her age was 25 years old or younger. After a short distance he pulled a 25-caliber pistol from his pocket then blindfolded her. He said he kept talking to keep her calm, while driving to a secluded place in Ottawa Park. He forced the victim to remove her clothes and he raped her on the seat of the car.

After raping and robbing the woman of a small amount of money, he had her get dressed and step outside of the car. He blindfolded her with her own scarf and then put the gun tightly against her heart and shot her.

"I always use small-caliber guns because they don't make much noise," he said. "I shot her at close range because there is less noise."

Cook actually sounded like he was proud of himself when he mentioned that fallen snow also muffles the sound of gunshots. As he continued, he gave the impression that he was enjoying telling us how he robbed, raped, and murdered the victim.

"I think I shot her only once because I remember her falling as soon as I shot her." "I left her lying in the snow and drove off. I felt the snow would soon cover the body so I didn't try to hide the body. I really never tried to conceal any of my victims," Cook said.

Later, after getting home, he said he heard the news and the reporter said the victim had been shot with a .25-caliber pistol and that the police had found tire tracks near where the body was found.

"So I wouldn't get caught, I dismantled the weapon and threw it away in different sections of the city, so the police wouldn't find it and perform ballistics on it," he said, claiming he also changed all four tires on his Pontiac so police couldn't compare the treads with the treads found at the scene.

Other than the fact that Cook thought he only shot Vicki Lynn Small one time in the heart – she was actually shot twice in the chest and four times in the head – Cook's description of the murder was accurate.

* * * * *

The next homicide Cook described was that of Stacy Balonek and Daryl Cole, both 21. Cook abducted them while they were parked in front of Stacy's house on Doyle Street. It was after 2 a.m. Sunday, Aug. 2, 1981, and Cook was driving around in his pickup truck.

"I was alone when I spotted them sitting in the car talking. I parked my truck nearby and approached the car on the passenger side where the girl was. I asked for directions, giving an address I knew was in the vicinity of where they were parked. Usually when people think you are just looking for an address, they don't become alarmed and they will make an effort to help you locate the address."

"Once the girl rolled the window down and became cooperative, I pointed my .22 pistol at them and slid into the front seat of the car. I wanted to get off the street so I wouldn't be noticed by anyone. I directed the man to drive to a secluded place in the area where I tied his hands with his belt and I tied the girl with something, but I don't recall what I tied her with. I wanted to restrain the man because he is the power, and once you have the power controlled you are in control. I put both people into the trunk of the car then drove to some railroad tracks under the Central Avenue overpass.

"I removed the girl from the trunk," Cook continued. "I untied her hands and made her undress and lay across the hood of the car. I had the .22 gun in my hand and I was holding it to the side of her head. 'Please,' she cried, 'if you don't hurt me I will do anything you want.' The girl was too scared to resist and the man was tied up in the trunk. I had sex with her on the hood of the car then made her redress."

After retying the girl's hands, he said he made her get on her knees while he opened the trunk of the car. He told the man to get out of the trunk and kneel beside his girlfriend.

"I didn't want to use the gun to kill them because I had used the gun before. I didn't want to leave the same M.O. as I did in the other murders for fear that the police would easily trace the killings to me."

Cook found several baseball bats in the car trunk.

"I made him kneel beside his girlfriend then I hit him so hard with the baseball bat that his head struck her head, knocking her unconscious. After they were down, I continued hitting both of them over and over again until I could be sure they were dead."

"Once I was sure they were dead, I untied them, and then I opened the trunk and stuffed their bodies inside. I didn't want to leave anyone tied up because the police would pick up on that M.O. The belt I had tied the man's hands with was all bloody so I walked down the railroad tracks and threw it into a wooded area. I drove the car back to the area where I had left my truck and abandoned the car. I parked it on a street that ran parallel with Central Avenue. I then drove off in my own truck."

* * * * *

As Cook continued his confession of the murders, he seemed mesmerized. He enjoyed relating his exploits as if he considered the victims his trophies. Instead of shame and sorrow, he appeared excited and proud. He seemed eager to tell about his next victims, Denise Siotkowski and Scott Mouton in March, 1981.

The couple had left the Centre Market on Navarre Avenue in Oregon, a small suburb of Toledo. Both were employed by the store and had just gotten paid, heading out to eat and socialize. They would not be seen again until their bodies were found in the trunk of Ms. Siotkowski's Oldsmobile by Oregon police.

After an apartment dweller became suspicious of Ms. Siotkowski's abandoned car and the police were called, the car was found on April 3, 1981, parked in a car port at the Fountain Circle Apartments.

Cook started by saying two of his sisters, Iris Evans and Hazel Madison, lived at the Fountain Circle Apartments. He visited them and on this night, as he was leaving alone, he noticed a car parked alongside the apartment buildings. The car was occupied by a young man and woman who were around 25 years old.

"I parked my pickup truck and got my .22-caliber pistol from the wheel-well where I kept it hidden. This was the same gun I used in some of the other murders.

I always kept it wrapped in plastic so the weather and salt from the roads wouldn't corrode it.

"As I approached the car, I saw that the girl was behind the wheel and the man was sitting on the passenger side. I tapped on the window and at first the man would not roll down the window. I hit the window with the gun and he finally rolled it down."

Cook laughed at the fact the man thought the window would protect them.

"I reached in and unlocked the passenger side door. I got into the front seat and the three of us were together. I made the girl drive to a secluded place where I tied the man's hands with his belt, then forced him into the trunk. I believe I might have tied his feet with a sweatshirt I found in the trunk. I either raped the girl on the hood of the car or on the front seat of the car. I preferred raping the girls outside the car because if someone came it would be easier for me to run and escape. The girl kept talking about her car and seemed to be more worried about the car than herself."

Cook said he thought this was funny because he was going to kill her afterward and she would never see her car again.

"After I raped the girl I made her get dressed, then tied her hands and placed her into the trunk with her boyfriend." The man, in an attempt to gain Cook's confidence, said he wouldn't attempt to escape and told Cook that his belt had come loose from his hands. Cook retied the belt around his hands.

Cook then took the .22 and emptied it into the bodies of the couple.

"I shut the trunk and drove to another isolated location. Car lights were approaching me from time to time so I had to be careful where I stopped," adding that he always had to worry that the oncoming cars lights could be that of a police car.

"As I drove I reloaded my revolver with six more shots and when I found a secluded alley or area where I felt safe, I again stopped. I opened the trunk and emptied my gun into the bodies for a second time. I wanted to make sure the victims were dead and that they didn't live to tell on me. I had made the mistake of accidentally leaving (Sandra Podgorski) alive and I promised myself I would not make that mistake again. I stole money from both the girl and man. The girl had $200 and the man had $100. I noticed that the car had an expensive stereo in it and I unhooked it so I could take it with me. I drove the victim's car back to the apartments and backed into a carport."

"I took the stereo and money and went to my truck. Before I left I also took the items I used to tie the couple with, not wanting any evidence left behind for the police to analyze. After I left the parking lot, I thought better about keeping the stereo from the girl's car. I wiped the fingerprints from it and threw it into a dumpster behind a Radio Shack."

"I know this is how people get caught, and I know that you should never keep anything stolen from your victims. You should never keep jewelry or anything that can be identified and traced to you."

* * * * *

192

Cook next described the murder of 18-year-old Connie Sue Thompson. She had left her home on Peck Street January 3, 1981, around 2 a.m. She had a fight with her boyfriend and had cut her wrist before running out of the house. Her sister said she wasn't severely injured but she felt she might have walked to nearby St. Vincent's Hospital for treatment. Connie Sue was not seen again until found by two young girls in a concrete culvert under Bancroft Street in western Lucas County. She had been raped, stabbed multiple times and strangled. Her body was found fully dressed.

Cook said his brother, Nathaniel, was with him during this murder. He said he again was driving his pickup truck when they spotted the young white woman walking on Cherry Street near St. Vincent hospital. He said the girl was either hitchhiking or just walking in the street and it was snowing. He asked her where she was going and she said she was going to the hospital because she had cut her hand or arm. Cook said they offered to take her to the hospital and she agreed, getting into the truck. She sat between the brothers.

"We drove toward St. Vincent's, but when we went past the hospital the girl protested. We shoved her down on the floor so no one could see her struggling with us. We drove out into the country where we both had sex with her on the front seat of the truck because it was too cold to do it outside of the truck. We took money from her but I don't remember how much."

"After we had sex with her, I believe Nathaniel suffocated her with a plastic bag but I can't recall for sure how we murdered her. I know she was not shot to death. We didn't want the body to be found so we dragged the body down a hill and hid the body under a small bridge. It was a small concrete bridge."

Cook gave an accurate account of Ms. Thompson's abduction and disposal of the body but he was wrong about the method of death. She had been stabbed and strangled with an unknown ligature. The ligature could have been a plastic bag and Cook could have thought his brother used the bag to suffocate her, when actually he strangled her with it. He also could have gotten the method of death confused with another murder, perhaps even one we didn't know about.

Sometimes, after so many murders, the killer will get some facts mixed up and sometimes they don't admit everything they have done, for one reason or another. If there were more than one killer involved, the other may not always know what his accomplice did.

Cook gave the impression that he didn't think there was anything wrong with robbing, raping and killing. He talked about the savage killings without any signs of caring or remorse. He liked what they had done and was proud of it.

All of these crimes were heinous and listening to Cook brag about how he and his brother murdered was sickening.

* * * * *

Perhaps the most horrifying murder, to me, was that of Dawn Backes, 12.

Dawn had been to a local kids' hangout near her home on February 21, 1981.

Her parents had gone to visit friends and Dawn was supposed to get a ride home with a girlfriend's father. The father didn't show up and Dawn started walking home a little after midnight. She vanished and was not seen again until two men looking for collectibles in the old abandoned State Theater on Collingwood found her in the basement on Feb. 25, around 8 p.m. She had been tortured, raped and violated with a piece of pipe. After the sadistic torturing, Dawn's head was smashed with a cinder block.

Cook said he was coming from work when he saw a young white girl walking on Bancroft Street just east of Secor Road. He was alone in his truck and he thought she was a college girl because she was walking on the same side of the street where the University of Toledo is located. He drove by her a couple of times to see if she was going to enter the campus area.

Much to his pleasure, Cook described how the girl continued walking east on Bancroft Street. She passed the campus and a short distance later she turned onto a side street. He sped up and turned onto the next street which was parallel to the street the girl had turned onto. He raced down the street until he knew he was ahead of her then he parked the truck near a short street that connected the two parallel streets. He reached into the right passenger's side door panel and unhooked the door lock so no one could open the door from the inside. You could open it from the outside, but not from the inside, he said.

"I walked down the short street to the street parallel to the street I had parked my truck on, and as I looked to the right I could see the girl hurrying down the street in my direction. I didn't want to scare her and have her scream, so I stayed to the far side of the sidewalk, giving her the impression that I was going to walk past her. I passed her without looking at her, but as soon as she passed me I swung around and grabbed her from behind. I held her by the waist with both arms so if anyone looked out they would think we were lovers. It was cold and dark out so it would be hard for anyone to see what was going on."

Cook described how he took the girl back to his truck and forced her into the truck on the passenger's side. Once inside she could not escape because he had locked the door from the inside. He made the girl get on the floor of the truck and covered her with a coat.

"I drove to Mayne Kynard's apartment on Maplewood because I knew my brother, Nathaniel, would be there. Mayne lived in the upstairs apartment. I parked in front of Mayne's apartment and saw my other pickup truck, Nathaniel had borrowed. I called up to the apartment but I didn't use names for fear someone would hear. I walked on the porch and rang the doorbell. Mayne came to the upstairs porch and I asked him if he was there, meaning my brother."

"Nathaniel came downstairs alone while Mayne stayed upstairs. Mayne never knew I had abducted the girl and had her in my truck. After Nathaniel came downstairs I told him about the girl I had in my truck. I drove the truck I had the girl in and Nathaniel followed in my other pickup truck. I decided to take her to the abandoned State Theater on Collingwood because we had been stripping the building of copper and selling it. When we were stripping the theater of copper I had to invest in some walkie-talkie's because the building was so big. I could talk to Nathaniel and we could also warn each other if the police came."

"We drove to the old State Theater and I parked while Nathaniel went to the theater side door and opened it. I then took the girl from

195

my truck and walked her down a ramp to the door. Inside the theater we took the girl to the basement. The theater was dark and I used my six-volt flashlight to see with. I always keep the flashlight in the truck. Nathaniel also had a flashlight."

"We took the girl into a side room in the basement. We made her take her clothes off and I had sex with her. After I was through Nathaniel had sex with her. I made her put her clothes back on when we were done. Then I struck her with my fist. She fell down and I picked up a cinder block and threw it at her head. I did not have my gun so I used the cinder block. She was still making noises and gurgling in her own blood, so I picked up the cinder block and hit her again. I wanted to make sure she was dead so I rolled the cinder block over to Nathaniel so he could hit her."

"To make sure it didn't look like she was raped I took a pipe I found nearby and I hit her deliberately between the legs to make the blood flow in the vagina area. I may have broken the pelvic bone. I did this to discredit any evidence that could be found there."

I asked Cook if anyone besides Nathaniel had helped him strip copper from the State Theater. He said Kynard helped him one time when Nathaniel wasn't around.

Cook said he had four bundles of 80-foot-long by 1-1/4-inch wire and it was too large to manage by himself. On this one occasion he had Kynard help him load it into his pickup. He said he sold the copper wire at a place on Hill Avenue that he couldn't remember the name of, but it was on the right-hand side as you drove toward the country. He said it was by the railroad tracks. Asked how many times he'd been in the theater, Cook said about 20 times. He knew the inside pretty well, the basement and attic and all over the building, because he had to trace the wire from one part of the theater to the other.

Cook said after raping and killing the girl in the theater, he and Nathaniel went home. He acted as if it was all in a day's work.

* * * * *

Cook was asked to tell about the murder he and his brother were arrested for after the DNA testing. This was the first murder in the series that investigators were aware of when the series of murders started. Cook said that the first murder was really that of Vicki Small on Dec. 20, 1973. I didn't have that murder on my list because it occurred seven years before the series we investigated started.

Cook cleared this up by saying he went to jail for a robbery after murdering Vicki Small, so the murders didn't continue until he got out of prison and murdered Thomas Gordon and assaulted Sandra Podgorski. They had been sitting in Thomas's car parked in front of Sandra's house on May 14, 1980, just after midnight. Two black men broke the passenger side window and forced their way into the car while armed with a .22 caliber rifle.

The victims were driven to Rabb Road in western Lucas County where Thomas Gordon was shot to death and Sandra Podgorski was raped. Gordon's body was stuffed into the trunk of his car and on the way back to Toledo Sandra was stabbed multiple times in the chest area and left for dead. The car and the bodies were abandoned in a secluded and remote area of north Toledo.

Cook said he and Nathaniel were together in his truck "when we did this one. We were riding around looking for victims when we saw a different couple in a white car. They were stopped for a train and we were behind them. We thought about abducting them but then we decided not to." Apparently, they felt it was too risky to follow the couple while looking for an opportunity to assault them. I thought, those young people will never know how close they were to becoming victims.

Cook continued that he and Nathaniel drove around for awhile searching for other victims. He said they saw Sandra Podgorski and her boyfriend parked on the street in the boyfriend's car.

"I parked my pickup truck and we forced our way into the white couple's car. Nathaniel had a .22-caliber rifle."

"Where did you get the rifle?"

"I can't recall, but I may have gotten it from Mayne Kynard; he gave me the .22-caliber pistol used in some of the other assaults and murders. I drove to an alley where we tried to force the man into the trunk. He refused to go into the trunk, so we let him sit in the back seat with Sandra. I drove out the expressway on I-75 and told

Nathaniel to watch for four-wheel drive vehicles and trucks because they set up high and could look down into the car and see the victims. I exited the expressway on Central Avenue. I drove to Dorr Street, then west on Dorr. I drove out into the country and parked alongside a road."

"We got the man out of the car and were talking to him when he ran. I told Nathaniel to get him and to shoot him so he didn't get away. Nathaniel pursued the man and I heard several shots. Nathaniel came back to the car and we took turns raping Sandra. I raped her first on the back seat of the car, then Nathaniel raped her. She got redressed on her own. I never redressed any of the lady victims after we raped them, I always made them get dressed before we killed them so it wouldn't look like they were raped."

"We stuffed the man into the trunk of the car and left the girl in the back seat. I sat in the back seat with Sandra while Nathaniel drove. On the way back to Toledo to get my truck, I stabbed Sandra multiple times with an awl. I thought I had killed her."

"Nathaniel drove to where my pickup truck was parked and I retrieved it. I used my pickup truck during all the murders and assaults, with the exception of the Sawicki murder; then I used my wife's car. The only reason I used her car that night was because my radio in the truck wasn't working at the time."

"Once I got my pickup truck, Nathaniel followed me. We drove to an alley where we abandoned the couple's car and dumped their bodies."

"Did you steal anything from the victims?"

"I took a CB radio but decided not to keep it so I threw it into a creek in the country. We may have gotten some money, but I can't recall how much."

"Did you steal any jewelry from Sandra or from any of your victims?"

"I never stole jewelry because it can be traced," he said.

"Did Nathaniel steal any jewelry from Sandra or anyone else?"

"I don't think so, but he could have."

"Did you take the keys from the car when you left?"

"No, I wouldn't have any need for them."

We always asked perpetrators if they stole anything from their victims for two reasons. First, the admission of stolen property leads to evidence they committed the crime. By being able to identify the property stolen from the victims implicates them. Secondly, it is important to make every effort to recover the victim's property for them or their loved ones.

"How did you find out that Sandra Podgorski didn't die? Did you hear about it from the media?"

"No, I think Nathaniel told me she had survived."

This is one of the reasons Cook always "over killed" his future victims; he wanted to make sure there would be no other witnesses. He was street smart, he knew if there were survivors they would tell.

"What happened to the .22 rifle Nathaniel shot Thomas Gordon with?"

"I cut it up with my acetylene torch. I had to spend $11 at a place on Hill Avenue to purchase a new tank of gas for it, then I could cut the gun up. I cut it into small pieces. I even cut the barrel in half, down the center; then I cut it into little pieces so ballistics could not be done on it. After I cut it up I took the small pieces to several different remote areas in the country where I walked into the woods and stomped the small pieces into the ground."

They had left a witness, but there would be no gun to prove they committed the murder. While in prison, Cook had received lessons from other inmates on how not to get caught, and he was implementing what he had learned.

* * * * *

It had been a long morning so everyone took a break. When the confessions continued, Cook talked about Cheryl Bartlett and Arnold Coates. Cheryl had walked up to the Kroger Store at South and Broadway on Jan. 27, 1981, around 12:30 a.m. to meet her boyfriend, Arnold. He worked for Kroger's, and they were going to walk to their apartment after he got off work.

As they walked home, they were confronted by a black man armed with a .22 pistol. They were forced down an alley to a vacant garage and met by a second man. They took turns raping Cheryl while Arnold was held at gunpoint.

Cheryl was robbed of a set of wedding rings and a watch.

Arnold was robbed of a watch and his wallet containing $2.

Before the robbers fled, one of them made Cheryl and Arnold hug each other tightly, and then the gunman shot Cheryl in the back. It appeared he only had one bullet in the gun because she was shot just once. Apparently the would-be killer thought the bullet would pierce the girl and the man, killing both. The bullet entered the girl's body but did not exit and continue into the boyfriend. Cheryl Bartlett would survive but was severely injured.

Cook didn't remember this incident very well, or for some reason he didn't want to talk much about it. He said he and Nathaniel were in his pickup truck when they spotted the couple walking in Toledo's South End. Cook said he got out of the truck while Nathaniel went to park it, and he confronted the couple armed with the same .22 revolver he later used in some murders and assaults. He directed the couple down an alley where he found a vacant garage.

"I took the couple into the garage and was joined by my brother. Apparently Nathaniel had seen me force the couple into the garage before he parked the pickup truck. We both raped the girl. I recall taking a watch from the man but later threw it away because I was afraid that it would be traced to me. The watch had a dent in it and I felt it was traceable."

"Did you take a set of wedding rings from the girl?" Cook was asked.

"I don't recall taking any rings, but if I did I threw them away. If you tried to get the rings or any jewelry appraised so you could sell it, the appraiser could tell on you. After this assault, I decided not to keep any traceable jewelry or property."

"I didn't feel this couple would tell on us, so I was going to leave them alive in the garage. I sent Nathaniel to get the truck and then I made the couple hug. As I started to leave, I accidentally shot the girl."

From the evidence in this case it didn't appear that the shooting of Cheryl Bartlett was any accident.

* * * * *

Cook next told us about a rape where he let the victim go.

"I was walking around looking for someone to rob late at night on Bancroft Street near Parkside when I saw a short white girl about 25 years old pull up to the curb. I hid behind trees and cars watching her get out of her car on the driver's side. The girl had a bag and placed it on top of the car. Before she could close the door I wedged her between the car and the driver's door. I forced her back into the car and locked the passenger side door. I put the bag back into the car and drove to a nearby alley."

"The alley was lonely. I forced her to have oral sex with me. You never know about forcing oral sex, especially when you have a gun, because they might think you are going to kill them anyway and you might not have junior any more. After talking to the girl for awhile, I felt she would not try anything foolish, and that she would not tell on me."

"We talked a long time and she told me she was a dental hygienist. By her demeanor, I felt she was sincere and wouldn't tell on me. I decided not to hurt her and I drove back to the area from where I had abducted her. I parked a short distance away so she would have to walk a distance, giving me time to wipe the car clean of my fingerprints and to flee to my pickup truck I had parked nearby.

"The girl told me she had not lived in the area very long and said, ' How do I get back to my house?' I told her which way to go and she left the car. I told her that I would leave the key in the car and she could get it later. I wiped the car clean, then ran to my truck."

Cook said there was another white woman he raped but didn't kill. She was coming from Church's Chicken or another fast food place. He abducted and raped her but let her go. He also robbed a man coming from a bar one time but didn't kill him. The man only had $2 and hadn't seen his face, so he let him go.

Cook said all these crimes were after he and Nathaniel raped Sandra Podgorski and murdered Thomas Gordon. He said Nathaniel killed Gordon with the .22 rifle and he used his .22 pistol during some of the other murders and assaults.

Frank P. Stiles

* * * * *

Cook was shown a photograph of murder victim Lorena
Zimmerman, 18, who was abducted on Aug. 29, 1981, while
leaving Kip's Night Club in West Toledo. Her nude body was found
in a field off Westwood by the Conrail railroad tracks. She had been
raped and strangled. The field was behind Kripke-Tuschman
Industries, a business where Anthony and Nathaniel Cook sold
copper wire and other metals.

Cook was asked if he recognized the nude girl. He looked at the
picture a long time, then said he didn't think so. He was asked if he
ever left any of his victim's nude. Cook said even though he made his
victims get dressed after the rapes, and before killing them, the one
he and Nathaniel left under the bridge in the snow may have been left
nude. He said he couldn't recall for sure. He was describing the
murder of Connie Sue Thompson, but he was mistaken because she
was found fully dressed, lying face down and partially frozen.

Cook was advised that Lorena Zimmerman was found nude in a
field near Kripke-Tuschman Industries, where he and Nathaniel used
to sell their copper wire and other metals. He was told that this
business was near Hill and Westwood. Cook was shown photographs
of the murder scene. He was told the girl was covered with a piece of
plywood.

Cook said he never covered up any of his victims. He seemed
confused about the details of the two murders. Since he talked of a
possible victim that may have been left nude, he and his brother can't
be ruled out for the murder of Zimmerman, but neither can this
homicide be cleared. Both murders had the same modus operandi.
The brothers sold their copper wire and other metals at Kripke-
Tuschman located near where Zimmerman's body was found, and she
had been abducted and murdered in the same manner as Connie Sue
Thompson, who Cook admitted killing.

* * * * *

The next murder Tony Cook was asked about was that of Mark

202

Wiler, 34, who lived in Flint, Mich., but on Aug. 17, 1981, had gone to a wedding in Columbus.

After the wedding, Mark left for home but never made it. His body was found in a grassy area near the Norfolk and Western railroad tracks in North Toledo. He had been bludgeoned to death. His wallet and car were stolen and the car turned up back in Columbus near where Nathaniel Cook lived at the time. The murder was committed close to where Anthony Cook lived and in the same general area where Janie Fall was assaulted and Stacey Balonek and Daryle Cole were murdered.

Cook said he didn't know about this murder. Even though there is insufficient evidence to clear the case, I believe the Cook brothers are still good suspects in the case. Cook may be reluctant to talk about it because the murder could be prosecuted in either Columbus or Lucas County. He knew that the Lucas County prosecutors can only give him and his brother immunity in Lucas County, and this could have led him to deny the murder.

* * * * *

Even though I didn't think there was much possibility that the Cook brothers were the ones who abducted the missing Cindy Anderson on Aug. 4, 1981, during daylight hours, I again questioned Cook about the case. He denied any involvement but said that while driving through Dayton he saw a missing person poster of her.

I showed Cook a picture of a young white girl; the picture was found in Nathaniel Cook's trunk at the home of Mayne Kynard. Kynard told me that Tony Cook wanted him to get rid of this picture because police would be very interested in it. "Do you know who this girl is, Tony?" I asked.

Cook looked at the photograph and said he didn't recognize her, nor did he remember telling Kynard to get rid of the picture. He did admit, however, that he knew Nathaniel kept the trunk at Kynard's apartment and that both he and Nathaniel kept things in it. The reason I asked Tony about the photograph of the girl was because I felt she might be a murder victim we had not tied to Cook.

* * * * *

Cook was asked about the attempted abduction of 18-year-old Janie Fall as she walked home from work June 22, 1981. She was grabbed by a black man who pulled her down a hill toward a wooded area. The assailant struck her on the face and body but she managed to break free and run.

Janie identified Anthony Cook as her assailant at the line-up on Oct. 15. She also identified a photograph of Cook's pickup truck. Cook was indicted for the abduction.

Cook remembered an incident like this, but said when he grabbed the woman; he believed he took her down an alley. A man on his porch was watching while the lady started screaming and fighting with Cook, so he let her go and ran. He was afraid the man on the porch would call the police or come help her.

* * * * *

Cook went on to say he also remembered confronting a young white couple in their car while he was wearing a ski mask and armed with his .22 pistol. While he was trying to force his way into their car, a man came out of a house, so he ran.

This was the assault on Charles Hackenberg and Laurie Specht as they were parked in front of Laurie's house on July 23, 1981. I held a line-up for this case and both victims identified Anthony Cook as their attacker. Cook was indicted for aggravated robbery in connection with this case. The line-up they viewed was the same one Janie Fall, Leslie Sawicki, and Todd Sabo viewed after I arrested Cook for the Peter Sawicki murder on Oct. 14.

* * * * *

The last murder discussed with Anthony Cook was that of Michelle Hoffman, 19. Michelle was the niece of police investigator Tom Ross and was last seen by her boyfriend on Sept. 2, 1981, at around 3 a.m. She was waiting in her boyfriend's car for him to get off work at the Columbia Gas Company in downtown Toledo. Her boyfriend discovered her missing at 7 a.m. when he got off work. She was later discovered bludgeoned to death on Sept. 17, around 6:30 p.m., in a wooded area behind Mulberry Park. This is in the area where Tony Cook lived and frequented. It was not far from where some of the other victims were abducted and murdered.

We decided Sgt. Forrester should question Cook alone about this case. We felt Cook may be reluctant to talk about the case in the presence of Tom Ross because the girl was Tom's niece. It was also felt Cook might not want to discuss the case with me because I had arrested him originally for the Sawicki murder and it was thought he might hold a grudge against me and hold back. We wanted to clear all the cases and in this case it was important to bring closure to Tom and his wife Sonia.

Tom and I watched by way of the close-circuit TV located in an adjacent room.

Forrester went over the details of the case with Cook. Maps were drawn of the location where the body was found so Cook would know exactly where the body was discovered. We didn't want to give Cook any reason to forget about this case.

Cook denied this murder but, again, wasn't convincing.

Later, when reviewing the video/audio tape of Cook's interrogation, I noticed that after everyone except Cook had left the interviewing room, he appeared very nervous and started talking to himself. It sounded to me like he was saying; "I should of let her go." A short time later it sounded like he said to himself, "No, they won't do that, they won't do that." I felt Cook was talking about Michelle Hoffman because she was the last victim he was asked about. I felt he might now be sorry he did not let her go because of the pressure we were putting on him to admit his guilt. After hearing those remarks and along with the modus operandi Cook had used, I felt even stronger that Cook murdered Michelle Hoffman. I believed Cook might not want to admit to this murder because the victim was a homicide detective's niece.

Part of the conditions of the plea bargain was that Tony and

Nathaniel Cook could be subjected to a polygraph examination concerning any murder the investigators felt they may not be telling the truth about.

I suggested that Tony Cook be taken to the scene of the Hoffman murder, Mulberry Park, and shown the area where the murder was committed. After the tour was complete, Cook was to be given a polygraph examination. If Cook was the murderer we wanted to do everything possible to clear this murder.

The interview was concluded and a polygraph examination was arranged.

Toledo Police Division polygraph operator Bart Beavers administered the test to Cook on April 5. The examination was administered after Cook had been taken to the crime scene and shown the wooded area behind Mulberry Park, where Michelle Hoffman was murdered.

Anthony Cook was asked the following relevant questions, which he answered no to: "In your statement are you lying about some of the murders that you committed in Lucas County? Did you plan in advance to make a false statement today about some of the murders that you committed in Lucas County? Did you participate in the murder of Michelle Hoffman in Mulberry Park? Did you murder anybody in Lucas County other than who you have told us about? Are you deliberately lying about other Lucas County murders in an attempt to get your brother Nathaniel a deal?"

Cook's readings contained response inconsistencies and erratic tracing abnormalities on the relevant questions. Based on these PolyGram's, all questions with the exception of did you participate in the murder of Michelle Hoffman were ruled inconclusive. The PolyGram's did conclusively indicate that Cook was being deceptive when he said he did not participate in the murder of Michelle Hoffman.

The polygraph backs up my theory that Cook murdered Michelle. Otherwise, the results of the polygraph examination cannot clear Cook of committing the other homicides I suspect him of being involved in.

Nathaniel Cook's Confession

Nathaniel Cook was brought to the district station and interviewed by Tom Ross and I on April 3, at 2:28 p.m. Also present was his attorney, Peter Rost.

Nathaniel Cook first spoke about the murder of 12-year-old Dawn Backes, who was abducted after midnight, on Feb. 22, 1981. She was taken to the abandoned State Theater on Collingwood, where she was raped and murdered in the basement of the building.

"I was visiting our friend Mayne Kynard at his apartment on Maplewood when my brother Tony came over. It was dark and cold out but I don't recall the month. The doorbell rang and Mayne answered the door. Mayne came back and said my brother Tony was downstairs and wanted to see me."

"I went downstairs and as I walked outside Tony motioned for me to come over to his pickup truck. I got into the truck where I saw a young blindfolded white girl on the floor of the truck between the bucket seats. Tony drove and I was on the passenger's side. Tony drove to the abandoned State Theater on Collingwood, near Scott High School, where he took the girl out of the truck. Tony told me to park the truck while he took the girl inside the building."

"I parked the truck then entered the building. I called to Tony and he responded. I found him and the girl in the downstairs dressing area of the theater. We had flashlights because it was so dark in the theater."

"Tony told the girl to take her clothes off and then had sex with her. I had sex with the girl after Tony was done and then the girl got dressed. The girl was blindfolded during the rapes. I picked up a pipe and hit the girl in the head and she fell onto the floor. She wasn't making much noise but she was shaking and kicking. I then picked up a cinder block that had holes in it and dropped it onto the girl's head. I wanted to put her out of her misery. After I hit her with the cinder block she quit moving."

"Did Tony tell you to do this?"

"No, Tony didn't tell me to do this, I did it on my own."

"Were you high?" Cook was asked.

"I may have had some marijuana and may have been drinking some before the rape and murder."

Cook said when he does bad things he just blocks it out. "I don't want to remember so I just block it out of my mind," he nonchalantly explained.

"Did you steal anything from the girl?"

"I didn't and I don't know if Tony took anything from her or not. After we killed the girl we left the theater. I don't recall where we went, I may have had a vehicle that I was driving parked at Mayne's apartment, but I don't recall."

"Have you ever been in the State Theater before?"

"Oh, many times. We stripped the building of copper wire and any metals we could find to sell."

"Did Mayne know Tony had the girl in the truck?"

"Not to my knowledge."

"Did you ever tell Mayne or anyone else about the murder?"

"No I never did."

"Did Tony tell anyone?"

"Not to my knowledge."

"Did you see reports of the murder on the news or in the paper?

"It was reported, but I didn't read about it or watch the news myself. I didn't want to think about the murder."

* * * * *

Cook was next questioned about the rape and murder of Connie Sue Thompson, abducted at night from Cherry Street near St.Vincent's Hospital on Jan. 3.

Connie Sue was taken to Langenderfer Road in western Lucas County. There she was raped, stabbed multiple times with an ice-pick type weapon, and strangled. She was found abandoned in a culvert under the roadway. The victim was fully clothed, lying face down in the shallow frozen water.

"It was at night and it was cold and snowy out," Nathaniel said. "I had been drinking beer and was feeling high. I don't recall how we got her into Tony's truck or where we got her from, but I do remember she was a white adult girl with red hair."

"We took her to the country. I didn't rape her because I was too high. I don't remember if Tony raped her or if he took anything from her. I strangled her with a piece of wire. I can't remember if she had gotten redressed or not. I remember we took her from one location to another after I strangled her and I remember we put her in the back of the truck while covering her with a piece of canvas. We hid the body in a sewer-like concrete pipe under the road. I don't remember the exact location but it was in the country."

* * * * *

"Now, we want to ask you about the abduction, murder, rape and robbery you were arrested for."

This was the murder of Thomas Gordon and the abduction and rape of his girlfriend, Sandra Podgorski. They were snatched on May 14, 1980, around 12:30 a.m. from in front of Sandra's home on Utica Street. They were in Thomas's car when two black men broke the passenger window and forced their way into the car. One assailant drove Thomas's car while the other held the victims at gunpoint in the back seat of the car. Thomas and Sandra were made to lie on the seat of the car so outsiders couldn't see them.

The victims were taken to western Lucas County where Thomas was shot to death and stuffed into his car trunk. Sandra was raped by both killers, stabbed and left for dead. The car and bodies were driven back to Toledo and abandoned. Sandra Podgorski was left for dead but survived.

"Do you remember this murder?" Cook was asked.

"Yeah, the basics, It was night and we were driving around in Tony's pickup truck when Tony said, 'I see something.' We saw a young white couple parked and setting in the man's car. After Tony parked his truck and we got out, we saw a brick and Tony said, 'Get the brick and break their car window.' I broke the passenger window where the girl was sitting and we forced the couple into the back seat. I had a rifle. Tony drove the man's car to a nearby alley and forced the man out of the car. Tony attempted to make the man get into the trunk of his car but he refused. Tony finally gave in and let the man get back into the back seat of the car with his girlfriend."

"Tony drove west on the freeway and into the country. He stopped on a secluded side road and Tony made the man get out of the car. While Tony was having sex with the girl in the car, I held the man at gunpoint. The man grabbed the gun and we struggled for the gun. The gun went off and I shot the man three or four times."

"My brother got out of the car and looked at the man then we put him into the trunk of his car. We got back into the car with Tony in the backseat with the girl, while I drove back to Toledo. Tony was talking to the girl in the back seat, then he started stabbing her with what I thought was a knife. Tony said she's dead. I continued to drive back to Toledo and I drove to the near vicinity of where we left Tony's pickup truck. Tony got his truck and I followed Tony to the area of Ketcham Street where I parked the car in an alley."

Cook was asked if he or Tony took any property from the victims. He said he didn't take anything from them, and didn't know if Tony took anything or not.

"We thought both victims were dead, so we left in Tony's pickup truck."

"What happened to the rifle you shot Tom Gordon with?"

"It was Tony's gun and he took it."

"What were you wearing that night?"

"A green Army jacket, blue jeans, and a ball cap."

"What was Tony wearing?"

"A green knit cap," Nathaniel replied.

"Was it a ski mask or just a plain knit cap?"

"I don't know. He didn't pull it down so I don't know if it was a ski mask or just a knit cap."

* * * * *

Anthony told us about the abduction/robbery of Cheryl Bartlett and Arnold Coates and the rape and shooting of Bartlett.

After the rape and robbery, the victims were made to hug each other then one of the rapists shot Ms. Bartlett in the back, but she survived.

Cook was asked what he knew about this rape, robbery, and shooting.

"I recall that we were in Tony's pickup truck and we saw this white couple walking by an alley. As I recall we were going to rob the couple. I remember Tony telling me to go and get the truck but I don't recall raping anybody, or anybody hugging. I recall Tony telling me to go and get the truck but I don't remember anything else."

"Tony was in prison for long periods of time, wasn't he," Nathaniel Cook was asked.

" Yes, I didn't know Tony very well until he got out of prison."

"How did you get involved with Tony?"

"I don't know. I can't answer that."

"Did Tony ever tell you about the murders he committed without you?"

"No, we never discussed what Tony did by himself or even what we did together. I didn't want to talk about it. I didn't want to remember what we did, there was no glory in it for me and I can't speak for my brother."

"Were you ever involved in any cases where you were alone?"

"No, all the cases I was involved in, Tony was also involved in."

"Other than the cases we have discussed with you, are there any other cases that you have been involved in that we haven't discussed?"

"No, just the cases we discussed."

* * * * *

"How about a guy that had been tied to a tree near where Tony lived? He was found in the Greenbelt area, near New York and Joseph Streets. His car was taken from him and it was found in Columbus near where you use to live. His name was Mark Wiler."

"I don't recall anything about that and Tony never told me about a case like that. We never discussed what each other did or even what we did together."

"Did Tony tell you about the Sawicki case and that he was in trouble?"

"No, I was living in Columbus at the time and when I came to Toledo he never told me about the Sawicki case or any other cases that we weren't involved in together."

I showed Cook a Polaroid picture of a young white girl that I found in his green storage Army-type trunk, left at the apartment of Mayne Kynard. He said he didn't recognize it.

* * * * *

Cook was asked about the murder of Tom Ross's niece, Michelle Hoffman, who had been abducted on Sept. 2, 1981, and brutally bludgeoned to death behind Mulberry Park. Her body was found fully clothed and badly decomposed in a wooded area on Sept. 17, 1981, behind the park area. I described the area of the park and where the body was found.

Cook said he knew the area, recalling there is a cemetery next to the park and that the park is down in a gully or valley. He said he knew the area but he had never been down in the park itself.

"Did you have anything to do with her death?" Cook was asked.

" No, I don't know anything about that murder."

"Your brother never told you about it?"

"No, my brother and I never discussed what we did."

I asked Nathaniel where he and his brother sold copper and metal they stripped from vacant and abandoned buildings, and Cook mentioned Kripke-Tuschman Industries.

* * * * *

"There was a lady, Lorena Zimmerman, who was found behind Kripke-Tuschman Industries, raped and murdered. What do you know about that?"

Cook said he knew nothing.

I continued, asking whether Cook had driven trucks for his brother-in-law. He said he had, to Warren, Mich., Columbus, and down to Laredo, Texas. He said when he traveled long distances a man traveled with him, but he didn't remember the man's name. He said he never traveled with his brother and that they worked for different brothers-in-law. Responding to my next question, Nathaniel said he never picked up hitchhikers and didn't know if his brother, Tony, ever did.

I looked Nathaniel Cook in the eyes and said, "Nathaniel, I am sure your attorney has told you this, but I want to advise you again that everything you tell us now will be cleared up with no extra charges being placed against you. If you lie or hold anything back about other murders or assaults that you and or Tony have committed, and we find out about them, you can be charged. "Do you understand this?"

"Yes, I understand, and I have no other murders to tell you about."

I felt Nathaniel hadn't been completely honest and was holding back.

Particularly, I felt that Nathaniel may have been involved in the Mark Wiler case. Mark had been brought to Toledo from Columbus in his own car, then murdered. His car was driven back to Columbus from where he had been abducted and the car was found not far from where Nathaniel was living.

Coincidental - maybe.

After the interview, Nathaniel Cook was given a polygraph examination, where no deception was indicated. He was specifically asked about Michelle Hoffman's murder, but the names of the other victims were not mentioned. He was asked the general question; "Did you murder anybody in Lucas County other than who you told us about?"

There is insufficient evidence to clear any of the other murders Anthony and Nathaniel are suspected of having committed, but there is also insufficient evidence to eliminate them.

Since both Cooks drove semi trucks over the road in Ohio and other states, it is also possible that they may be involved in homicides in other states. When I interviewed their friend, Ernest Kynard, he told me that both brothers bragged about picking up white female hitchhikers. If this is true, there could be other homicides in Ohio and other states that these investigators don't know about.

The interview with Nathaniel Cook ended with my feeling that he had not been completely honest. This is not uncommon when dealing with murderers and other criminals. The bad guys rarely give it all up.

Chapter 27
The day of reckoning

It was April 6, 2000, and Judge Charles S. Wittenberg's courtroom was filled to capacity. This was the day of reckoning for the Cook brothers – they would be given their sentences. The few victims who survived the brutal, heinous assaults at the hands of Anthony and Nathaniel Cook, and the family and relatives of the victims who died, would be given a chance to speak their thoughts.

In accepting the plea bargain agreed upon by the prosecutors, defense attorneys, surviving victim Sandra Podgorski, families of the deceased victims, and the Cook brothers, Judge Wittenberg asked for their statements concerning the charges.

Anthony and Nathaniel continued to show no emotion or remorse as they each told their story of how they abducted Thomas Gordon and Sandra Podgorski while the couple was parked in front of Sandra's house in Thomas's car.

As the victims, family members, and spectators leaned forward, straining to hear every word, the Cook brothers told how they abducted the couple in Thomas's car, and then drove them to a secluded area in western Lucas County. There Anthony encouraged Nathaniel to shoot Thomas Gordon to death, and then they both raped Sandra.

While returning to Toledo, Anthony viciously stabbed Sandra multiple times with an awl, leaving her for dead. Thomas was dead in the trunk while the Cook brothers asked each other; "Do you think the bitch is dead?" As the killers escaped in the darkness, Sandra fought for her life. Frightened and in pain, Sandra survived and was in court to tell her story.

During their statements, the brothers didn't appear to be sympathetic to the victims or their families, trembling and sobbing nearby. After the statements, Judge Wittenberg accepted their pleas.

He found Anthony Cook guilty of the aggravated murder of Thomas Gordon and sentenced him to 20 years to life in prison. This sentence was to be served consecutively with the 20 years-to-life sentence he was already serving for the Peter Sawicki murder.

Judge Wittenberg found Nathaniel Cook guilty of the attempted murder of Sandra Podgorski and two counts of kidnapping. He was sentenced to 20 years in prison, with judicial release on Feb. 13, 2018. A judicial release is an agreed upon time the defendant is to serve in prison before he is released.

While the pleas were rendered and the sentences imposed, victims, family members of victims, and some close friends, stood ready to give their impact statements. For most, it had been almost 20 years since their loved ones were brutally assaulted or taken away. For the Vicki Small family, it had been almost 27 years. One could see many expressions and emotions on their faces as they waited their turn to speak. There was the look of hatred, disgust, relief and even the want for forgiveness.

When one human being takes the life of another for no other reason than lust, greed, or hatred, the community immediately feels the fear and agony of the victim. Those feelings are shortly endured but it is the inner emotional turmoil the family and loved ones suffer that last a lifetime. One by one they voiced years of emotional stress and an eternity of pain.

Most of the statements that followed were delivered to the court personally, but there were some who could not control their emotions so their written statements were read to the court.

Lattie Small Russell, the mother of Vicki Lynn Small, could

hardly speak her thoughts while trembling and shaking. With tears streaming down her cheeks she said her family members' lives had been shattered since that fatal day.

"How could any living thing do this?" she asked. "They can't be, they aren't human. Vicki's younger sister had to identify her body. I wish it were up to me to sentence you, but the law has its own rules. I cry every day and will until the day I die."

Vicki Small's brother, Rusty, was only 9 when she was raped and shot to death in Ottawa Park. Rusty said while growing up he saw the pain the death of his sister caused his family and that maybe the plea agreement would bring some closure to all of them. "We will never forget my sister, but it's so hard to talk about it," he said.

Thomas Gordon's sister, Doreen Powers, said a day never passed that her mother wouldn't cry and mourn her son's death. Trying to hold back her tears, she explained how her mother could visualize her son crying out after the first shot was fired into his body, 'Oh, my heart! My God, no!" As another shot broke the silence. She said her mother could see Thomas falling to the ground and dying.

Thomas's brother, Walter Gordon, a former Lucas County sheriff's deputy, spoke in his brother's behalf. Thomas was law abiding, dependable, considerate, and compassionate. The Cook brothers' acts characterized them as unfit to live in a benevolent society. These victimizers deserved the harshest punishment dispensable by the court, he said.

Sandra Podgorski Rollins wanted so badly to tell her story but was overcome by her emotions and the thoughts of that awful night. The prosecutor's office victim assistance program director, Joan Coleman, read Sandra's prepared statement while Julia Bates held the sobbing Sandra in her arms.

The statement read: "I cannot comprehend how people could brutalize, terrorize, rape, and destroy my life and the lives of so many others. You, Anthony and Nathaniel, have committed these violent acts, and for your actions you must pay your debt to society.

"I forgive you, a lot of people will not and cannot, but I couldn't live with myself if I carried the hatred you have carried with you for so long. This kind of hatred will eat a person alive, as it has done to you.

"These violent acts of crime you have introduced into my life are burned into my mind, heart, and soul. This is something you just don't let go of. You have burdened every single day of my life with guilt, the guilt of a survivor."

Bonnie Podgorski, Sandra's mother, spoke to the court through her prepared statement.

"Your Honor, I would like to start by reading a prayer. It is a prayer of parents for their teenage children.

"Dear Lord, be with us and our children now as they enter adolescence. Give them the courage to be different and not be compelled by the unthinking crowd as they develop strong loyalties toward their friends. Give them the strength to guide and control new physical powers as they grow and develop.

"Give them the reverence for their bodies and for the role in divine creation as they mature. Let the normal attraction between sexes be for them a further unfolding of your divine plan for life and love, and not a path of temptation or compromise. Give them also discernment, docility and patience, so that they do not become prideful and rebellious as they develop new powers of mind and a questioning spirit. Give us wisdom to realize that much of their behavior stems from change and confusion, and not disrespect. "Give us wisdom to know when to say yes and when to say no, when to forbid and when to forget, when to praise. And finally give us courage to let them go away from us as they grow in age and grace and wisdom before God, and man, under your care and your law, Amen."

Bonnie Podgorski continued, "This is the prayer that I as a mother of three teenage daughters prayed every night when my daughters were out and away from home."

This is the prayer that was prayed for my daughter, Sandra, and her friend, Thomas Gordon, the night we received the phone call that every parent dreads. I only wish, Anthony and Nathaniel, that your parents would have had that same prayer, that desire and that hope for you when you were going through those changing and confusing times during your adolescence. If they had, perhaps you would not be here and we as a family would not be here, but sadly and regretfully, that did not happen.

"We as a family are not here to judge or condemn you; that will be done by the One who is greater than we. Your plans to carry out your violent and evil acts against two innocent young human beings were meant to destroy and disrupt the lives of all those who loved them. God's plans were different and God's plans for his children will always prevail.

"Sandra was spared that night, not because it was your decision, but because it was his decision. As a family we have faced hardship and pain, joy and happiness, but through our faith and our love we have kept our family together and strong. We did not and will not ever let any forces of evil and hate destroy all that we have worked for, all that we stand for, all that we live for, and all that we believe in."

In conclusion, Bonnie Podgorski faced the Cook brothers and said, "I say to you, Anthony and Nathaniel, we as a family and the family of Thomas Gordon, we of this community, loving and law-abiding citizens, are the victors over all that you have done, and you are the losers. Now you have to endure the consequences of your evil deeds."

"I would like to say to my daughter, Sandra, that you are a brave and courageous woman. You have come forth to speak for those victims who have been silenced. You have given their families at least a bit of closure and the knowledge that justice has prevailed. Sandy, you are a hero and we love you."

Many thoughts flashed through my mind when the mother of 12-year-old Dawn Backes stood to speak. I thought of my own vivid nightmares over the years since Dawn's death and I thought of the hours spent with Sharon Backes Wright while listening to her pleas for information about possible suspects in the case. Many days I would show up for work at the police division and, soon after, Sharon would arrive. Her agony was my agony. She blamed herself as all parents do, and she missed her little girl as all parents would. Sharon loved Dawn so much it was eating her up inside.

Visibly shaken, Sharon stood before Judge Wittenberg.

"My name is Sharon Backes Wright and for 12 years I was

Dawn's mother. They murdered her and I am only supposed to have two to three minutes to tell you how I feel. Let me tell you exactly how I feel. I didn't have Dawn's final moments of life to tell her I loved her. The brothers had used the cover of darkness to hide their cowardly ways to snatch our innocent 12-year-old Dawn.

"They plea-bargained for their lives, but what if Dawn could have asked for another day?"

Sharon faced the Cook brothers, shook her fist at them and said, "I will never know how long you kept my little girl in that dirty theater basement, torturing and raping her."

She turned to Judge Wittenberg and announced, "Their ugly faces were the last thing Dawn saw on this earth, which must have seemed like an eternity for her."

Sharon continued, "Dawn was a kind and loving child, she was my only child. She was also an only grandchild. I cannot put into words the pain we have suffered. Why? My life will never be the same, no child, no grandchildren, because of these murderers."

"I have known for 19 years who these killers were," Sharon told Judge Wittenberg. I had told Sharon when I arrested Anthony Cook about my belief that Anthony and possibly his brother Nathaniel had murdered her daughter. I had told Sharon, "I arrested the right guy for Dawn's death when I arrested Tony Cook for the Sawicki murder."

Sharon continued that "these slimy creatures of the earth that took my most precious gift from God need to be flushed down the gutter. I have some peace of mind knowing that someday they will die also. They have a sure ticket to burn in hell and to meet the devil. I pray their fate will be to end up as Jeffrey Dahmer did. I hope they suffer the pain that they inflicted on Dawn that night."

The brother of Stacey Balonek, Mitch Balonek, spoke of confusion in his mind about what happened to his sister. Mitch, who was a teacher at Scott High School at the time, said he couldn't understand how anyone could be so evil that they would bludgeon his sister and her boyfriend, Daryl Cole, with a baseball bat. He continued that he and his family are still haunted with bad memories of the couple's brutal death.

Edith Csizmar, a friend of the Balonek family, who attended

Harmony Baptist Church with them, wrote the court a letter explaining how hard it was for the family following Stacey's death. She wrote, following Stacey's death in August 1981 that she herself got married in December. It was Stacey's father, Stanley Balonek, who walked her down the aisle. Edith continued that she knew he would have loved to have walked his dear Stacey to her future husband and watch her life grow with her own home and family.

From a written statement Daryl Cole's family said how pleased they were that the tragedies were finally coming to some sort of closure. They thanked prosecuting attorney Julia Bates and her office for the relentless pursuit in bringing the killers to justice. They continued that it is still hard to accept the fact that Daryl was gone. "We would feel more satisfaction if there was any clue as to why."

Hank Siotkowski spoke to the court on behalf of his family and his deceased sister, Denise.

"I never thought I would be standing before a court making this statement. Not many can imagine the pain and devastation this brutal crime has caused our family.

Denise was the last child to live at home and was a treasured companion for my father. She was a joy to be around, positive, outgoing, and you could always count on her.

"My family looked forward to dancing at her wedding, but instead we cried at her funeral. Her loss caused my parents to suffer severe depression, which my father never recovered from. He lost his will to live and died a few years later, a broken man."

Grief-stricken and emotional, Steven Moulton addressed the court, saying almost 20 years had gone by since his brother Scott's life was brutally taken.

"I still find it very difficult to put my feelings into words that can describe our family's loss without becoming verbally vicious towards the Cook brothers. 'Brother' being a key word, as that is what I lost and can never get back. There can be no punishment in this world that could repay my family or the rest of the families involved, for taking my brother's life and the lives of so many others. These two individuals have shown they have no respect for human lives, other than their own."

Steven sadly went on, stating that many people lost a special person and part of themselves at the hands of the Cook brothers. He said he wished that if only for a minute, these cold-hearted brothers could feel the agony and suffering of not only his family but the families of the other victims. Steven finished by saying, the senseless and selfish acts of their violence will surely be with all of the victims families for the rest of their lives.

Kelly Barton, the niece of Connie Sue Thompson, said Connie was only 18 when she was brutally killed. When life is taken by another, it is a tragedy, but when that person has not had the opportunity to really begin life, it's far worse.

"Connie never got to attend airline school and become a flight attendant as planned; she wanted to travel the world. She never got to have a career, get married or have children, all the things that make our lives complete.

"She was a surrogate sister to me, and I looked up to and admired her greatly. I cannot stress enough what a good person she was. She did well in school and was the first person in our immediate family to graduate. She knew what she wanted out of life, everyone loved her. Her positive impact on the world will never be erased, and she will never be forgotten by those who knew and loved her.

"Connie's mother had a heart attack when told of her youngest child's fate. Regretfully, she died before Connie's killers were found and she went to her grave with many questions and no answers. We now have the opportunity to see some sort of justice for Connie and the other victims. The value that these men placed on life is cheap and we feel their life should have no higher value than those they stole. These two men are animals and deserve nothing less than death themselves. Rabid and vicious dogs are put to sleep and they deserve the same."

Two of the survivors, Arnold Coates and Cheryl Bartlett, weren't present at the sentencing, but I contacted each of them later. I had been told that Cheryl was upset because her case was not prosecuted, even though she identified Anthony Cook after his arrest for the Peter Sawicki murder. I wanted to explain to her that her case was not presented to the grand jury because she was in the hospital at the time. I further wanted to tell her that we had every intention of prosecuting her case but were waiting until after the trial of Anthony Cook for the Sawicki and Sabo cases.

After Anthony Cook was convicted for those cases and sentenced, prosecutors decided to drop all the non-homicide cases. The reason was that the sentences for those cases would carry less than 20 years in prison, and since Anthony Cook received 20 years to life, it would not be practical to prosecute the remaining cases. I wanted to tell Cheryl and Arnold that we didn't want to put the victims through the stress of a trial, since Cook could receive no more time in prison if convicted for the added charges.

I contacted Arnold, also known as Bud, at his home and asked him what had happened in his life after the Cook brothers assaulted them. He and Cheryl broke up soon after the assaults occurred, he explained.

"The incident changed our lives and things have not been quite the same since," he said. Cheryl and their son, Erik, moved to Tennessee to live with an uncle, and Bud continued working for the Kroger Company. He was promoted to meat cutter, and at the time I met with him he still worked for Kroger's.

"I met my wife, Kim, shortly after Cheryl and I parted ways and we have a lovely daughter named Amber," he said. "Amber is now 22 years old and is about to graduate from college." I met Amber while at the Coates home.

Arnold continued, "I have never gotten over the assault and the awful things that occurred to Cheryl that night. I never told anyone about what happened and was able to keep my secret until The Blade wrote an article a few years ago about the series of homicides that occurred in Toledo during 1980 and 1981.

My name was in that article, and this is when my family and friends learned the truth.

"I never sought counseling, and I now have no sympathy for criminals. I think murderers should be given a year to complete their court appeals, then should be put to death. No one can really understand what those people have done to their victims and families unless one has been a part of that pain. I am a survivor, but my life and that of the ones I love, will never be the same."

When contacted by telephone, Cheryl Bartlett Fann was pleased to hear from me. I explained the reason for not pursuing her case through court and she said she was grateful that I had called to explain. She said she had always felt cheated out of her day in court. I asked Cheryl what had happened in her life since that awful night in January, 1981.

"Bud could never deal with what happened to us and we broke up soon after the assault. I moved in with my mother, Georgianna, and my stepfather Jack Depew. My stepfather was such a help and comfort to me during the time the baby and I stayed with them and even after I moved away. He would call and talk with me and was so kind and understanding. He passed away in 1998, and I miss his love and support.

"Mom tried, but she had a hard time coping with it all. Even though my parents were supportive I had to get out of Toledo and away from where it all occurred. I took my son, Erik, and moved in with my uncle in Tennessee. I have traveled back and forth to Toledo since, but I choose to live in Tennessee. I have had constant medical problems since the shooting and I have had 23 surgeries. I am suspicious of strangers and extremely nervous when coming into contact with black men. I can't force myself to go out at night alone, and I am always fearful.

"There have been many good things that have happened in my life. I now have three sons and am married to a wonderful and caring man, Danny Fann. I have four wonderful grandchildren and they reside near me in Nashville, Tenn.

It is with their love that I am able to deal with the past."

The encounters with Cheryl Bartlett and Bud Coates were an emotional experience for me, which brought back many unpleasant and sad memories. I thought, "May God bless Cheryl, Bud and all victims of violent crimes."

The surviving victims and the loved ones of those who did not survive have carried their hatred; want for vengeance and emotional stress for over 20 years, but will now finally have some closure.

A peaceful sign of relief surrounded those present after the sentencing and after all of them had the chance to tell about their feelings. They hugged and talked with one another, and a look of tranquility illuminated their faces. It was a sure sign that there is strength in numbers and now a bond that would last forever.

Leaving the courtroom, I thought to myself that, not all of the truth is known, and perhaps not all of the victims have been vindicated. But the pain for the future victims – those who would have surely followed – was stopped before the evil brothers could have ruined more lives.

Lucas County Prosecuting Attorney Julia Bates reviews Anthony and
Nathaniel Cook murder cases at their sentencing on April 6, 2000.

Cook brothers – Nathaniel left and Anthony right – at their sentencing.

Sharon Backes Wright, mother of 12 year old murder victim Dawn Backes, speaks her mind at Cook brothers sentencing.

Victim Assistant Director Joan Coleman assists surviving victim
Sandra Podgorski Rollins in giving her impact statement to the
court, while prosecutor Julia Bates comforts Sandra. Court Officer
Pete Sifuentes stands by.

LaVergne, TN USA
29 March 2011

222066LV00002B/54/P